Other Books by Michael Scantlebury

God's Eternal Plan
Understanding the Dual Aspects of Faith
Understanding the Revelation – An In-Depth Study
Are We Living in The End Times or The Last Days?
Fathers and Sons – An Unveiling
Heaven and Earth – A Biblical Understanding
My Ponderings
Understanding the Kingdom of God and The Church of Jesus Christ
Eschatology – A Biblical View
As It Was in the Beginning, So Shall It Be...
Daniel In Babylon – The Study Guide
Principles for Victorious Living Volume II
Principles for Victorious Living Volume I
Present Truth Lifestyle – Daniel In Babylon
Esther: Present Truth Church
"I Will Build My Church." – Jesus Christ
The Fortress Church
Called to be An Apostle – An Autobiography
Leaven Revealed
Jesus Christ The Apostle and High Priest of Our Profession
Internal Reformation
God's Nature Expressed Through His Names
Kingdom Advancing Prayer Volume III
Kingdom Advancing Prayer Volume II
Kingdom Advancing Prayer Volume I
Apostolic Purity
Apostolic Reformation
Five Pillars of The Apostolic

EXPLORING THE *Secrets* OF HIDDEN WEALTH

MICHAEL SCANTLEBURY

EXPLORING THE SECRETS OF HIDDEN WEALTH
Copyright © 2024 by Michael Scantlebury

Editorial Consultant: Anita Thompson – 604-521-6042
Question Section: Anoja Wijesuriya – 604-314-6605

All rights reserved. Neither this publication nor any part of this publication may be reproduced or transmitted in any form or by any means, electronic or mechanical, including photocopying, recording or any information storage and retrieval system, without permission in writing from the author.

All Scripture quotations, unless otherwise indicated, are taken from the Revised Standard Version. Copyright © 1946, 1952, and 1971 the Division of Christian Education of the National Council of the Churches of Christ in the United States of America. Used by permission. All rights reserved. All Scriptures marked KJV are taken from the King James Version; all marked NIV are from The New International Version; and those marked MSG are from The Message Bible and is used by permission.

Hebrew and Greek definitions are from James Strong, Strong's Exhaustive Concordance of the Bible (Peabody, MA: Hendrickson Publishers, n.d.).

Michael Scantlebury has taken author's prerogative in capitalizing certain words that are not usually capitalized according to standard grammatical practice. Also, please note that the name satan and related names are not capitalized as we choose not to acknowledge him, even to the point of disregarding standard grammatical practice.

ISBN: 978-1-4866-2636-6
eBook ISBN: 978-1-4866-2637-3

Word Alive Press
119 De Baets Street Winnipeg, MB R2J 3R9
www.wordalivepress.ca

Cataloguing in Publication information is can be obtained from Library and Archives Canada.

"Michael Scantlebury has the unusual skill of patiently sifting through Scriptures – almost like an archaeologist who wants to unearth historical and spiritual layers that will unfold the future.

"In his most recent work *Exploring the Secrets of Wealth* a process of discovery that began years ago – Michael threads that narrow place between a God who richly provides and contentment and avoiding the love of money.

"The principles in the book if applied precept by precept, will allow God – who owns everything – to manifest His Presence and generosity through you.

"It will discipline you into a mentality about God, wealth, self and others – and the nature and relationship between them – in the context of the Kingdom of God interjecting the systems of the earth."

Prophet Jacob John
Pastor – Acts 29
Vancouver, BC, Canada

"No doubt Apostle Michael Scantlebury is a wise master builder and Kingdom scribe whose writing breaks seals and unveils the Mind of God.

"In this masterpiece, he approaches a subject that has been quite controversial in some quarters, the subject of finances in the Kingdom. In his usual straight forward but yet biblical approach, Apostle diligently explained the parables of Jesus in view of provisions, delving into a strong theological framework for stewardship and how to form relevant partnership for wealth which is an effective interaction with the world system for material advance and contentment as a Kingdom virtue which in Apostle Michael's word is a 'correct heart position'.

"This book is highly recommended for Church leaders, churches, and Saints alike as it brings a biblical worldview and most importantly, a wholistic approach to the subject of finances and Kingdom economy. A book written from a pure heart to edify the Saints."

Maxwell E. Ogaga, Pastoral Overseer
Pastor & Bible Teacher,
God's Kingdom Advancement Ministries, Nigeria

"Apostle Michael Scantlebury is a prolific writer of Kingdom truth for this generation. His book *Exploring the Secrets of Hidden Wealth* is a must read for those seeking the fullness of God's promises and principles.

"The Lord going before us is key to opening up His providence and grace. In this book we learn the Lord calls us by our name and the specialness that this calling carries.

"We are stewards of God's possessions and His wealth is hidden for us, not from us. God has given us vision for provision placed in the miracles of Jesus in blessing His people.

"This book will expand your mind and bless your soul. I highly recommend it."

Apostle Michael Scott
Lighthouse Covenant Ministries
Youngstown, Ohio

"*Exploring the Secrets of Hidden Wealth* is a revelatory guide to understanding the power, purpose and stewardship of money.

"This is one of the most cutting-edge truths I've come across on the subject of Kingdom finances.

"This is a must-read!"

Apostle Alfred J Mochubela
Emmanuel New Life Centre
Toekomsrus, Randfontein, South Africa

"Michael Scantlebury an Apostle of the most high God has unveiled and unearthed a strong, practical word for the new day Church.

"The balance I find in this book is necessary to position the Body of Christ to the promise of possessing the Nations for the Kingdom God.

"Yes! God has promised to reposition and empower the Church to reach new heights of Dominion in the earth.

"This book seeks to expose and birth in us God's agenda and a new hunger into the purpose of God in this time.

"The inspiration and revelation expounded in this book is Timely, balanced, powerful and Prophetic.

"God is at work in the Church and in the earth and His will, shall prevail as His Kingdom will advance!"

Dr. Ben Christopher Don
Higher Height Christian Embassy
Kumasi, Ghana

"This book is a goldmine in bringing both balance and depth to the message of Kingdom prosperity and wealth to the Body of Christ.

"Apostle Michael Scantlebury takes us on a spiritual journey in exposing and breaking religious tradition while assisting us to connect with God's purpose, principles and processes in the areas of Kingdom prosperity and wealth management.

"Every chapter is filled with insights of wisdom and scriptural references that delivers great truths to the reader. I highly recommend this book as a necessary manual in helping us prepare for the wealth God is about to unleash upon His Church."

Apostle Chuks Ajuka
Fresh Fire Ministries and Oasis of Love Church
Mitcham, Bromley
United Kingdom

"We have known Apostle Michael Scantlebury for close to three decades and can say that we are thankful for his timely prophetic instructions and powerful insights received over the years. This book can also do that for you. We have known the author to be a man of passion and strong conviction whose genuine love and care for the Body of Christ is expressed through his apostolic ministry and literary works.

"The book served to fuel in us an even deeper personal search into God's intention for wealth among His people. It provides a unique perspective on God's heart towards us and His empowering ability, through resources, to bring His purpose to pass."

Apostle Dave and Pastor Marisse Cropper
Oikos Global Centre
Trinidad and Tobago

Contents

Introduction	xi
CHAPTER ONE **WEALTH**	1
CHAPTER TWO **JESUS' MIRACLES OF PROVISION**	5
CHAPTER THREE **DYNAMICS OF SOLOMON'S TECHNOLOGY OF BUILDING**	15
CHAPTER FOUR **THE ISSUE OF CONTENTMENT**	23
CHAPTER FIVE **THE DESIRE TO BE RICH**	27
CHAPTER SIX **THE RICH YOUNG RULER'S ENCOUNTER WITH CHRIST**	31
CHAPTER SEVEN **THE PARABLE OF THE TEN MINAS**	45
CHAPTER EIGHT **THE PARABLE OF THE VINEYARD**	55

CHAPTER NINE
PRINCIPLES OF WEALTH AND PROSPERITY - ONE   59

CHAPTER TEN
PRINCIPLES OF WEALTH AND PROSPERITY - TWO   69

CHAPTER ELEVEN
PRINCIPLES OF WEALTH AND PROSPERITY - THREE   81

CHAPTER TWELVE
PRINCIPLES OF WEALTH AND PROSPERITY – FOUR   89

CHAPTER THIRTEEN
UNDERSTANDING THE SIGNIFICANCE OF FIRSTFRUITS
    99

CHAPTER FOURTEEN
ANOTHER VIEW OF MAMMON   109

OTHER EXCITING TITLES   129

Introduction

Isaiah 45:2-3

I will go before you, And make the crooked places straight; I will break in pieces the gates of bronze And cut the bars of iron. I will give you the <u>treasures of darkness</u> And hidden riches of secret places, That you may know that I, the LORD, Who call you by your name, Am the God of Israel. [Emphasis Author's]

To whom were these words spoken? They were spoken to Cyrus, the king of Persia. You may be wondering, how did a heathen monarch named Cyrus come to be included in the Word of God for a future time. Cyrus, though a heathen King, was an instrument chosen of God to do an appointed work in a future time: He overthrew the great Chaldean empire by taking the city of Babylon, and restoring the children of Israel to their own land! Think about this!!! One hundred and seventy years before he accomplished and executed the tasks assigned to him, he was expressly declared by name in the Old Testament, the holy book of the Jewish people, in its record of inspired prophecy. This is a testament and proof regarding the inspiration of God's Word, and that every single event is under His divine appointment and control!

Not only was Cyrus called by name, but the very work which he had to do was declared long before the necessity arose for it to be accomplished. The man had not been thought of yet in his parents' life. He was not yet a sperm swimming for its destiny and yet the work for which he was raised up and divinely appointed, was already on the roster of God's to do list. Cyrus would deliver the two tribes of Judah and Benjamin after they were punished for their sins and were carried into captivity to Babylon for seventy years.

When the seventy years were up, this Babylonian captivity had to be reversed and that is when Cyrus came into the picture through the appointment of God to enable them to return.

This was a very great work for him to be called to do and execute, a work so great that he could not have performed it unless he had been supernaturally and specially aided by God. He did not have an arsenal, he was not a commander of a legion of warriors yet he had to take a city whose walls were fifty cubits thick and two hundred feet high, surrounded by a wide ditch full of water, and defended with one hundred gates of brass. The city was also well equipped with warriors and sentries and well provisioned. It was an impenetrable city so strong and powerful as to defy every mode of attack then known. If the Lord, therefore, in the words of the Bible, had not "gone before him;" if He had not "broken to pieces the gates of brass, and cut in sunder the bars of iron," Cyrus could never have taken that mighty city, but would have been utterly defeated in the attempt.

This clearly explains the literal meaning of the text. But we also must consider the greater and extensive application. The promise, it is true, was given to Cyrus, and we know it was literally fulfilled; but are the words applicable only to Cyrus? Have we no fortress to take, no city of salvation to win? Do we not need the Lord to go before us, and make our crooked places straight? Have we no gates of brass, no bars of iron, which shut out approach and access, and which we need the Lord to break in pieces and cut asunder for us?

Does the road to Heaven lie across a smooth, grassy meadow, over which we can quietly walk in the cool of a summer evening and leisurely amuse ourselves with gathering the flowers and listening to the warbling of the birds? Unfortunately it is not so!

No child of God ever found the way to Heaven a flowery path. That path is the wide gate and broad way which leads to perdition. Instead, it is the straight gate and narrow way, the uphill road, full of difficulties, trials, temptations, and enemies, which leads to Heaven. If then, we are

Zion's pilgrims, heavenward and homeward bound, we shall find the need of such promises, in their spiritual fulfillment, as God ordained and executed for Cyrus. This idea may give us a clue to the spiritual meaning of our text. I shall, therefore, with God's blessing, endeavor to take this experimental view of it, and interpret it as applicable to God's family, omitting further reference to Cyrus, except as it may help to elucidate the spiritual meaning. Considering it, then, in this light, I think we are able to observe in it three special features:

1. What I may perhaps call God's preliminary work, in "going before His people, making for them crooked places straight, breaking in pieces gates of brass, and cutting asunder bars of iron."
2. The gifts which the Lord bestows upon them, when He has broken to pieces the gates of brass, and cut asunder the bars of iron, here called "treasures of darkness and hidden riches of secret places."
3. The blessed effects produced by what the Lord does thus gives—a spiritual and experimental knowledge, that "He who has called them by their name is the God of Israel."

God's preliminary work in "going before His people, making for them crooked places straight, breaking in pieces gates of brass, and cutting in sunder bars of iron." Before I enter into God's preliminary work, and show how it all stands on the firm footing of promise, I must drop a remark or two on the characters to whom these promises are made. To make this clearer as well as more personal, we will look at it in the singular number, as God has worded it – "I will go before *you*." It is evident from the very language of the text, that the promises contained in it are given to the exercised child of God, and to him alone. No one else, therefore, has any business with or any spiritual interest in it. Consider this point a moment for yourselves before I proceed further. Let this point be firmly impressed upon your mind, that if you have no spiritual exercises, trials, or temptations, you have at present, no manifested interest in the promises made in the text; nor can you enter spiritually into their suitability and beauty, or know for yourself the divine and heavenly blessedness, which is lodged in them. But if, on the other hand, you are a tried, and exercised child of God, one who knows the plague of your heart, and the many difficulties and perplexities which beset the road to

Heaven, you have reason to believe that you are one of the characters to whom these promises are addressed.

1. The first promise, as it is the sweetest, so it lays a foundation for all the rest—**"I will go before you."** But look at the words. Have you ever considered what they imply? How great those difficulties are which need the God of Heaven and earth Himself to go before us in order to overcome them! Surely, they must be insuperable by any human strength if they need nothing less than the immediate presence and power of the Almighty Himself. Go out some fine evening and look at the sky, spangled with thousands of stars, and then say to yourself, "What, do I need the same Almighty hand which created all these glittering orbs to go before me?" Now, suppose that at present, as regards religious matters, you have never encountered a single trial, temptation, or difficulty; but have found everything easy, smooth, and a matter of course, and have never met with one obstruction, which you could not by some exertion of your own remove. If matters be so with you, how in the world can you need the Lord to go before you? You could not, I would think, except by way of compliment, presume even to ask for such a favor.

But if, on the other hand, you are contending with great inward perplexities of mind, feel to be in much soul peril and sorrow, and are surrounded by difficulties which you cannot surmount by any strength or wisdom of your own, and yet surmounted they must be, then you will feel a need for the Lord "to go before you." There is nothing that we are more averse to than trials and afflictions in providence or grace, and yet, if truth be spoken, we never come to know anything aright or receive any real blessing without them. Usually speaking, the Lord does not appear in providence or grace, or make Himself known in love and mercy to the soul, except in the path of trial. We must, therefore, go into trials and afflictions to learn not only the end, but the very beginning of our Kingdom journey.

If we, then, are rightly taught, we shall feel a need for the Lord to go before us, not only now and then, but every step of the way, for unless led and guided by Him, we are sure to go astray. How strikingly was this the case with the children of Israel. How the Lord went before them every step from Egypt to the Promised Land, marshaling their way night and day in the cloudy pillar! How, also, He went before them after they reached Canaan, and made the hearts and hands of their enemies as weak as water so that they could offer no resistance to their victorious arms. How the very walls of Jericho fell, as it were, of their own accord, and how the Promised Land was almost conquered before the children of Israel set foot upon it! So must the Lord go before us step by step.

But you may apply this promise to a variety of things. It is applicable not only to spiritual but to temporal trials and perplexities – to His going before us both in providence and grace. If the Lord goes before, preparing the way and opening a path for us to walk in, all is well; every difficulty at once disappears, every mountain sinks into a plain. But if we cannot see nor feel Him going before us, then no ray of light streams upon the path, no friendly hand removes the barriers. Beset behind and before, we know not what to do. It seems as if we were thrown back upon ourselves—miserable refuge enough, and we know not what step to take.

But the words apply not merely to the Lord's going before us in afflictions and trials and removing them out of the way, or giving us strength to bear them, but also to the manifestation of His Holy and Sacred Will. There are few things more trying or perplexing to a child of God than to desire to do what is right, yet not to know, in particular circumstances, what is right, or if known how to do it; too long to learn the Will of God in some important matter, and yet be unable to discover plainly and clearly what that Will is. In this case, when brought into some extremity, the Lord sometimes goes before in His kind providence by unexpectedly opening a door in one particular direction and shutting up all others, intimating thereby that this is the way in which He would have us walk; and sometimes in His grace by whispering a soft word of instruction to the soul which at once decides the matter.

But it is especially in the removal of obstructions that the Lord fulfils this part of the promise. This was especially true in the case with Cyrus, in whose path such formidable obstacles lay. What these are we shall more clearly see by passing on to the next portion of the promise.

2. **"And make crooked things straight."** This promise springs out of the former, and is closely connected with it; for it is only by the

Lord's going before that things really crooked can be straightened. But what if there are no crooked places in our path, no crooked places; what if the road we are treading is like an arrow for straightness, and a turfy lawn for smoothness? Why, then we have certainly no present interest in the promise. It does not wear a smiling face; it does not stretch out to us a friendly hand. But on the other hand, if we find such crooked places in our path, that we cannot possibly straighten in our own might, such rough and rugged spots that we cannot smooth them, the promise given that the Lord will go before us and straighten them for us affords us much hope.

But what is meant by crooked places, and where do they come from? Generally speaking, we can say that these crooked places diverge into two paths. Some are inherently crooked, that is the way they are, they cannot be interpreted as anything else—and others are not so obviously crooked, but God has an appointment ordained for someone where His might will be shown.

The things which are **crooked in themselves**, that is, inherently and necessarily bent and curved, are so through sin; for sin has made crooked that which was originally straight. Thus crooked tempers, crooked dispositions, crooked desires, crooked wills, crooked lusts and many other things are in themselves inherently crooked, due to being bent out of their original state by sin. They no longer lie level with God's holy will and Word. The man regenerated in the image of God who strives to live a holy life will detect the crookedness and contrariety in their own souls under heavy groanings of conviction

But there are crooked places in the path of God's family, which are not inherently crooked which are not necessarily sinful in and of themselves, but are **crooked on purpose by the hand of God to us, but they always have greater purpose in the long run.** Afflictions in body and mind, poverty in circumstances, trials in the family, persecution from superiors or ungodly relatives, heavy losses in business, bereavement of children, and countless and vast varieties of circumstances curved into their crooked shape by the hand of God, which are then "crooked things" handed to us.

Now, the Lord has promised to make "crooked things straight." Taken in its fullest extent, the promise positively declares that from whatever source they come, or of whatever nature they be, the Lord will surely straighten them. By this He manifests His power, wisdom, and faithfulness.

But HOW does He straighten them? In two ways, and this according to their nature. **Sometimes He straightens them by removing them out of the way, and sometimes not by removing them, but by reconciling our minds to them.** We have perhaps a crooked path in Providence. It may be poverty, persecution, oppression; it may be family trials or temporal difficulties; and this springs out of, or are connected with, circumstances over which we have no control. These crooked things we may frequently have tried to remove or straighten with our own might, but all our attempts to do so leave them as bad or even worse than before. Rebellion, peevishness, or self-pity may have further added to the churning of our minds in all of this which will in turn make those crooked paths more crooked than ever until such time we can't handle it and we are obliged to have recourse to the Lord. Now then is the time for Him to appear and fulfill His own promise, which He does sometimes **by removing the crooked paths altogether, taking us out of those circumstances which make them crooked to us, or putting an end to the circumstances themselves**. In this way the Lord sometimes makes crooked places straight. This was evident with Jacob, when He delivered Jacob from Laban's tyranny and Esau's threatened violence, and to David when He took Saul out of the way. Therefore health given for sickness, a deliverance in providence, a removing of an enemy out of the way, a bringing us from under the power of the oppressor, are all means whereby these crooked things are straightened.

But there is another way, a less popular and more painful way that none of us would prefer. And that is where the trial is not removed, but we overcome it by **bending our will to submit to it.** We must not think that the Lord will, in answer to prayer, remove all our temporal afflictions. So far from that, we may have more and more of them to our dying day. How then, it may be asked, can He fulfill His promise that He will make crooked places straight, if He leaves some of our worst crooked paths as crooked as before? He does it by bending our will to submit to them; and this He accomplishes sometimes by favoring the soul with a sweet sense of His blessed presence; and sometimes by throwing a secret and sacred light upon the path that we are treading, convincing us thereby that it is the right road, though a rugged one, to a city of habitation.

When the Lord thus appears, it brings submission – and as soon as we can submit to God's Will, and the rebellion, peevishness, and unbelief of our carnal mind are subdued, a sweet and blessed calmness is felt in the soul. The crooked place now at once vanishes as being melted into the Will of God. It is in this way, for the most part, that those places which are inherently crooked are made straight. There is no change in the things themselves, but in our views of and feelings towards them.

In a similar manner, the trial in providence which was crooked is crooked still; the people we have to deal with; the circumstances we have to encounter; the cross we have to carry; the burdens we have to bear, all remain unchanged and unaltered; but the Lord gives strength to endure the pain and trouble caused by them – and while they are borne in submission to His Holy Will, their weight is taken off the shoulders, and their crookedness is not so keenly felt. See how this was the case with those three eminent saints, Job, David, and Paul. Job's trials, David's bereavement, and Paul's thorn were all as before; but when the Lord appeared, Job repented in dust and ashes, David arose from the earth and anointed himself, and Paul gloried in his infirmities.

3. But the Lord also promised Cyrus in the text that He would, by going before him, **"break in pieces the gates of brass, and cut in sunder the bars of iron."** Cyrus longed to enter into and take possession of the city of Babylon; but when he took a survey of the only possible mode of entrance, he saw it firmly closed against him with gates of brass and bars of iron. These effectually barring all progress, he could not achieve the object of his desire. They were continually before his eyes, too strong for all his weapons of warfare; and unless battered down or broken to pieces, he could not capture the city.

Now can we not find something in our own personal experience which corresponds to this feeling in Cyrus? There is a longing in the soul after the attainment of a certain object, say, such as an obtaining of everlasting salvation, or a winning of Christ and a blessed experience of revealed pardon and peace, or an inward personal enjoyment of the sweet manifestations of God's favour and love. This, we will say, is the object the soul is set upon to attain, the Lord Himself having kindled these desires in the breast. But when, in pursuance of this object, we press forward to obtain it, what do we find in the road? Gates of brass and bars of iron. And these insuperable obstructions so stand in the path that they completely block up the road and prevent all access to the enjoyment of the desired blessing. It is, then, by the removal of these obstacles that the Lord fulfils His promise—"I will break in pieces the gates of brass, and cut in sunder the bars of iron."

Look for instance at our very prayers. Are not the Heavens sometimes brass over our heads, so that, as Jeremiah complains, "they cannot pass through"? No, is not your very heart itself sometimes a gate of brass, as hard, as stubborn, and as inflexible? So the justice, majesty, and holiness of God, when we view these, dread perfections of the living Jehovah with a trembling eye under the guilt of sin, stand before the soul as so many gates of brass. The various enemies too which beset the soul; the hindrances and obstacles without and within that stand in the path; the opposition of sin, satan, self, and the world against all that is good and Godlike—may not all these be considered "gates of brass," barring out the wished-for access into the city?

But there are also, besides "bars of iron." These strengthen the gates of brass and prevent them from being broken down or burst open, the stronger and harder metal giving firmness and solidity to the softer and weaker one. An unbelieving heart; the secret infidelity of the carnal mind; guilt of conscience produced by a sense of our base and innumerable wanderings and backslidings from the Lord; doubts and fears often springing out of our own lack of consistency and devotedness; apprehensions of being altogether deceived, from finding so few marks of grace and so much neglect of watchfulness and prayer—all these may be mentioned as bars of iron strengthening the gates of brass.

Now, can you break to pieces these gates of brass, or cut in sunder the bars of iron? That is the question. Could Cyrus do it literally? He had doubtless a large and valiant army, soldiers of the most approved valour, and possessed of all possible skill in the use of their weapons; but before them there stood the gates of brass and bars of iron. He might look at them in all their depth and width; but looking at them would not remove them. He might wish them broken asunder and cut to pieces; but wishing would go a very little way towards making them fall asunder. There they still were standing before his eyes, insuperable, impenetrable.

So with the feelings and experience of the child of God. There, right in his very path, the insuperable obstacles stand. He can no more break down his hardness of heart, darkness of mind, unbelief or infidelity than Cyrus could break to pieces the gates of brass of ancient Babylon. He can no more subdue the workings of a deceitful and desperately wicked heart than the King of Persia could by drawing his sword cut asunder at a stroke the bars of iron which strengthened the gates of brass. Here then, when so deeply needed, comes in the suitability and blessedness of the promise. "I will break in pieces the gates of brass, and cut in sunder the bars of iron." The words, spiritually taken, mean of course the removal of all hindrances that block up the road. Let us see, how hindrances dealt with by the Hand of God are soon to be hindrances no longer.

Look for instance at the holiness and justice of God which as pure attributes stand arrayed against the soul's entrance into Heaven and glory. How, it may be asked, are these to be removed? Can God part with any one of His eternal and glorious attributes? Can they be, as it were, disannulled and cease to exist? No; that is clearly impossible; but with regards to the heirs of salvation, they can be so dealt with to the point where they are no longer gates of brass and bars of iron to shut them out of Heaven. When Jesus by His sufferings and death, and by His meritorious obedience and divine sacrifice satisfied God's justice by glorifying the Law and making it honourable, He opened an entrance for His people into the City of God. Thus the Apostle speaks of His "blotting out the handwriting of ordinances that was against us, taking it out of the way, and nailing it to His cross." In this sense the Law, which is the reflection of God's justice and holiness, was broken to pieces as a gate of brass, and cut in sunder as a bar of iron; in other words, it stands no longer in the way as an insuperable bar to the salvation of the soul.

But if we look at the gates of brass and bars of iron as shadowing forth other hindrances, we shall see them not figuratively in this way, but actually broken down and smashed into pieces. Thus ignorance, unbelief, infidelity, hardness of heart, darkness of mind, guilt of conscience, and every other gate and bar, are at once broken asunder when the Lord dissolves the heart by the sweet application of love and His atoning blood. So the various temptations and besetment from without and within which seem arrayed against the soul, all disappear at once when touched by the finger of God; no matter how strong, deep, or high an iniquity is, there is not one that does not fall to pieces before the word of His mouth.

4. **The gifts which the Lord bestows upon them**, when He has broken to pieces the gates of brass, and cut in sunder the bars of iron, here called "treasures of darkness and hidden riches of secret places." But when, by the breaking down of the bronze gates, and cutting asunder the bars of iron, Cyrus got admission into the city of Babylon—and **what did he find there?** Countless treasures. Of these he at once took full possession, as the Lord's own free gift; for the promise ran, "I will give you the treasures of darkness, and hidden riches of secret places." Cyrus did not get hold of "the treasures of darkness," nor did he lay his hand upon "the hidden riches of secret places," which were stored up in the cellars of the king's palace, until he got into the city of Babylon through the broken gates.

Now look at this spiritually. Before your eyes in the dim distance is the city of salvation—the city which the Lord has blessed with every spiritual blessing. See how its towers rise in the horizon, and how the sun gilds its domes and palaces. But see how the same sun gleams upon the gates of brass thickly bound with bars of iron, and look how those shut out all entrances. But the Lord goes before, cuts in sunder the one, and breaks in pieces the other, and gives the soul a blessed entrance into the city.

5. Now what does He then and there manifest, and of what does He then put in the believer's possession? First, **"Treasures of darkness!"** But is this not a strange expression? "Treasures of darkness!" How can there be darkness in the City of Salvation of which the Lord the Lamb is the eternal light? The expression does not mean that the treasures themselves are darkness, but that they were **hidden in darkness until they were brought to light**. The treasures of Belshazzar, like the bank bullion, were buried in darkness until they were broken up and given to Cyrus. And in a spiritual sense, are there not treasures in the Lord Jesus? Oh! what treasures of grace there are in His glorious Person! What treasures

of pardon in His precious blood! What treasures of righteousness in His perfect obedience! What treasures of salvation in all that He is and has as the great High Priest over the House of God!

Yet all these treasures are "treasures of darkness," so far as they are hidden from our eyes and hearts, until we are brought by His special power into the city of Salvation. Then these treasures are not only brought to light, revealed, and made known, but the soul is at once put into possession of them. They are not only seen, as the Treasury clerk sees notes and bounds, but are by a special deed of gift from the Court of Heaven given over to him who by faith in the Lord Jesus receives Him into his heart. No one has the least conception of the treasures of grace that are in the Lord Jesus until he is brought out of darkness into God's marvelous light, and knows Him and the power of His resurrection by the sweet manifestations of His presence and love.

But the word "treasures" signifies not only something laid up and hidden from general view, but in the plural number expresses an infinite, incalculable amount—an amount which can never be expended, but suffices, and suffices, and suffices again for all needs and for all believing newcomers and established believers as well. When we get a view by faith of the Person and work of the Lord Jesus, and see the ever flowing and overflowing fullness of His Grace, it may well fill our minds with holy wonder and admiration. When we get a glimpse of the virtue and efficacy of His atoning blood, that precious blood which "cleanses from all sin," and that divine righteousness which is "unto all and upon all those who believe," what treasures of mercy, pardon, and peace are seen laid up in Him! To see this by the eye of faith, and enter into its beauty and blessedness, is indeed to comprehend with all Saints the length, and breadth, and depth, and height, and to know something of the love of Christ which passes knowledge. The sun will cease to give his light, and the earth to yield her increase; but these treasures will still be unexhausted, for they are in themselves infinite and inexhaustible.

6. But the Lord promised also to give to Cyrus **"the hidden riches of secret places,"** that is literally, the riches of the city which were stored up in its secret places. I believe Cyrus collected on the wealth of the city, but this also has a spiritual and experiential meaning

as well as the rest of the text with which it is connected to? Yes! Many are "the hidden riches of secret places" with which the God of all grace enriches His believing family. Let's consider the word of God. What hidden riches are stored up in its secret depths! Every promise is worth a thousand worlds! And we see clearly how every portion of inspired truth is filled to overflowing with the richest discoveries of the wisdom and goodness of God. But these riches are hidden from view. They lie concealed from the very vulture's eye in "the secret places" of revealed truth. Most people look for the heavenly lottery, they at times follow the Lord due to the erroneous teachings of the prosperity preachers…But when the Lord is pleased to bring the true treasures forth to the eyes and heart of any one of His believing children, it makes them say, "Oh, I could not have believed there was such fullness and depth in the Word of God, or such a sweetness and preciousness in the promises. And of course until it was brought to light and set before my very own eyes could I have conceived there was such beauty in Jesus, such love in His heart, such virtue and efficacy in His atoning blood, nor such joy and peace to be felt in believing. I could not have believed there was such power in the Word of God to wound and to heal, to cast down and to lift up. Oh, how the Word of truth in the hand of the Spirit surpasses not only every conception, but every anticipation of the heart. Oh, how these riches of secret places surpass all earthly wealth, and exceed in value thousands and millions of gold and silver.

But it is only as these hidden riches of secret places are opened up to the soul that we see or feel, or know what the Lord Jesus Christ is to those that believe in and love His Holy Name. It is this bringing forth of the hidden riches of secret places which stamps a divine reality upon God's Word, and makes it to be spirit and life to the soul. To feel the power and blessedness of these things is a part of that "secret of the Lord which is with those who fear Him;" and it is by getting into these blessed secrets, handling these treasures, and obtaining possession of these riches, that we come experientially to realize what a blessed power there is in a divine heartfelt religion. We may see the doctrines plainly enough in the Word of God; but if that be all we know about them, it is like seeing money which is not ours, and casting up accounts of other people's property. The grand point is not only to **see** the riches, but to be put in **possession** of them. A religion without power, without savor, without a felt blessedness in the truth of God, by the application of the Spirit, is worthless both for time and eternity. The real money is not in the sums represented on paper in a bank account, but rather in the cold hard cash in hand.

Now let's dive deep into how the promises are connected with "crooked places," "bronze gates," and "iron bars," and how the Lord goes before to remove them out of the way. Without this previous work we would be ignorant to our dying day of "the treasures of darkness;" we would never see with our eyes, nor handle with our hands, "the hidden riches of secret places." There are but few, comparatively speaking, who know anything of the sweetness and reality of a God-taught religion; of the power of grace upon the soul, or of the riches which are stored up in the fullness of the Son of God. Most even of those who profess the truth are satisfied with a name to live, a sound creed, a consistent profession, and admission to church membership, without knowing or desiring to know anything of the blessed reality of communion with God, of a revelation of the Lord Jesus, of the manifestation of His love and mercy to the soul, and the sealing of the blessed Spirit on the heart.

7. **The blessed effects** produced by what the Lord does and thus—a spiritual and experiential knowledge. Now what springs out of having these treasures of darkness brought to light? A spiritual experience and a knowledge of God, and that He is the God of His people—"That you may **know** that I, the Lord, who calls you by your name, am the God of Israel."

Think on the following expression, **"I, the Lord, who calls you by your name."** How special is this! What an individuality it stamps on the person thus addressed! How it makes religion a personal thing! When God singles out a man by name, it implies that he has special dealings with Him, and that he personally and individually knows Him. This stands firmly for the believer.. How many, for instance, are here reading this book whom I have never met. If I were to meet you in the street, not knowing you, I could not address you by name. But there are others known to me by name whom I can call by name when I meet you, from having a personal acquaintance with you.

Is it not so in God's grace? said he is known "to call His people by name," when by a special work of grace upon their heart, He calls them out of the world to a knowledge of Himself. He does not always speak in an audible voice, but the effect is as distinct as if He were to say, "John," or "Mary, I want you." We do not expect to see the same light, or hear the same audible voice which was manifested for Saul of Tarsus who later became the Apostle Paul, but we must experience a measure of the same power, and feel something of the same divine influence. When God calls a man, he will come as the power He puts forth cannot and will not be resisted—it is impossible to do so! It is certainly grace invincible, if not grace irresistible. He does not call us vocally as the Lord Jesus Christ called His disciples when He said, "Follow Me," but the effect is still the same.

Blessed be God, then, for all our trials and temptations. As James says – "Count it all joy when you fall into diverse trials;" and blessed be God for every burden and every exercise; and above all things, blessed be God for His grace which supports the soul in, comforts it under, and eventually brings it out of all its trials, where tears are wiped from every face!

At this point, let us now embark on uncovering this wealth that is stored up in hidden and secret places.

Hold on for one of the greatest rides of your life!

CHAPTER ONE
WEALTH

As we go into this series on Wealth let me state some foundational truths that will set the stage for this book's teaching. We all need to come to terms with the following foundational concepts of biblical finances. I will outline twelve of them (there are many more):

1. God owns all things. This includes the physical universe and all spiritual beings good and bad. God's ownership includes planet Earth, all living things, the people, their ideas, their gifts and capacities and the entire world's wealth, hidden and revealed.
2. We actually own nothing. The righteous angels, the devil, all fallen angels and demons also own nothing.
3. The idea of human ownership is a powerful deception. Actually, all we really have is temporary possession and control of the things that God owns.
4. God requires us to be responsible and account for how we handle His property that He places in our control. We owe nothing to God but thanks because Christ has paid for our indebtedness at Calvary.
5. Failure to understand the above concepts and to consistently apply them produces inadequate resources. The world's system of finance is built on the human responses that a lack of adequate resources creates, chiefly fear in the form of anxiety and greed.

6. God's financial system is higher than the world's financial system. It is built on hidden abundance.
7. Most of God's resources are hidden in Christ but available to all who wish to walk as Christ's servants in the realm of finances.
8. Entering into God's system of finances requires faith in Christ and releases abundant resources and the inner quality of peace.
9. Giving all resources away on command of Christ reveals a true application of spiritual financial understanding. Failure to pass this test is why many do not experience the supernatural in finances. This is a key concept that is neglected in most teaching on finances. Absence of this concept produces financial teaching that appears shallow, greedy and selfish.
10. God entrusts His things and His wealth to Christ's special tested servants who are genuinely and acutely aware that they own nothing. They are properly called *stewards*.
11. A faithful and tested *steward* will see ongoing supernatural increase and unusual supernatural intervention by Christ in his or her finances.
12. The lifestyle that lives by the truth that God owns all things and human beings own nothing is then called *stewardship*.

THE MEANING OF STEWARDSHIP:
The word *steward* or forms of this word are used frequently in the New Testament. The Greek word translated *steward* is *oikonomos* which is a composite word coming from *oikos* meaning *house* and *nemo* meaning *arrange*. The literal meaning of the word is *the one who arranges the house*. The word in the First Century denoted a manager of a household or estate. These managers or stewards were slaves or freemen but were never owners of the property that they managed.

Jesus and the early Apostles clearly taught on this powerful truth quite extensively. Here are a few examples:

> Please understand this balance; we are sons and friends of God, but we are also servants, stewards or slaves of Christ, and as such we will be called upon to give account to our Master!

Luke 16:1-17

He also said to His disciples: "There was a certain rich man who had a steward, and an accusation was brought to him that this man was wasting his goods. So he called him and said to him, 'What is this I hear about you? Give an account of your stewardship, for you can no longer be steward.' "Then the steward said within himself, 'What shall I do? For my master is taking the stewardship away from me. I cannot dig; I am ashamed to beg. I have resolved what to do, that when I am put out of the stewardship, they may receive me into their houses.' "So he called every one of his master's debtors to him, and said to the first, 'How much do you owe my master?' And he said, 'A hundred measures of oil.' So he said to him, 'Take your bill, and sit down quickly and write fifty.' Then he said to another, 'And how much do you owe?' So he said, 'A hundred measures of wheat.' And he said to him, 'Take your bill, and write eighty.' So the master commended the unjust steward because he had dealt shrewdly. For the sons of this world are more shrewd in their generation than the sons of light. "And I say to you, make friends for yourselves by unrighteous mammon, that when you fail, they may receive you into an everlasting home. He who is faithful in what is least is faithful also in much; and he who is unjust in what is least is unjust also in much. Therefore if you have not been faithful in the unrighteous mammon, who will commit to your trust the true riches? And if you have not been faithful in what is another man's, who will give you what is your own? "No servant can serve two masters; for either he will hate the one and love the other, or else he will be loyal to the one and despise the other. You cannot serve God and mammon." Now the Pharisees, who were lovers of money, also heard all these things, and they derided Him. And He said to them, "You are those who justify yourselves before men, but God knows your hearts. For what is highly esteemed among men is an abomination in the sight of God. "The law and the prophets were until John. Since that time the kingdom of God has been preached, and everyone is pressing into it. And it is easier for heaven and earth to pass away than for one tittle of the law to fail.

The basic concept of stewardship is revealed in the following.

- The rich man represents God as the owner
- The steward represents a Christian, who has control (not ownership) over the owner's possessions and in this case was squandering them
- Christ calls this steward an unrighteous steward because he was supposed to be taking care of the owner's property and was not— we will be exploring this in more depth later as we go deeper into the financial teachings of Jesus.

Here is another passage in which Jesus uses the concept of a steward to represent the Christian:

Luke 12:42-43

And the Lord said, "Who then is that faithful and wise steward, whom his master will make ruler over his household, to give them their portion of food in due season? Blessed is that servant whom his master will find so doing when he comes.

In our next chapter we will be exploring Jesus' miracles of provision.

LET'S CHECK OUR UNDERSTANDING OF CHAPTER 1: WEALTH?
1. How many foundational concepts of Biblical finances does the author discuss in this Chapter?
2. What are some of these concepts that resonated with you? Why?
3. How will you describe stewardship?
4. What are the meanings of the two Greek words that make up composite word Oikonomos?
5. What is the word used for 'oikonomos' in the English translation of the New Testament?
6. According to the author "we are sons and friends of God, but we are also servants, stewards or slaves of Christ, and as such will be called upon to give account to our Master!". Do you agree? Why or why not—Explain.
7. What are the basic concepts of stewardship as revealed in Luke 16:1-17?
8. Can you state another Scripture where Jesus likens the Christian to a Steward?

CHAPTER TWO
JESUS' MIRACLES OF PROVISION

As we continue our study of tapping into the source of hidden wealth, we will now look at Jesus and the miracles of provision that He worked while on earth!

FIRST MIRACLE
The Wedding Feast at Cana–John 2:1-11

> *On the third day there was a wedding in Cana of Galilee, and the mother of Jesus was there. Now both Jesus and His disciples were invited to the wedding. And when they ran out of wine, the mother of Jesus said to Him, "They have no wine." Jesus said to her, "Woman, what does your concern have to do with Me? My hour has not yet come." His mother said to the servants, "Whatever He says to you, do it." Now there were set there six waterpots of stone, according to the manner of purification of the Jews, containing twenty or thirty gallons apiece. Jesus said to them, "Fill the waterpots with water." And they filled them up to the brim. And He said to them, "Draw some out now, and take it to the master of the feast." And they took it. When the master of the feast had tasted the water that was made wine, and did not know where it came from (but the servants who had drawn the water knew), the master of the feast called the bridegroom. And he said to him, "Every man at the beginning sets*

out the good wine, and when the guests have well drunk, then the inferior. You have kept the good wine until now!" This beginning of signs Jesus did in Cana of Galilee, and manifested His glory; and His disciples believed in Him.

Who was present at this first miracle?—There was Jesus of course, His first five disciples (John 1:29-51) and Mary, His mother. The Bible was careful to let us know that they were invited guests.

Some Interesting Points to Note:

- Jesus' presence to perform a miracle at the wedding feast reveals the Father's approval of marriage
- At this stage of His ministry Jesus only had 5 disciples (five is the number of the Holy Spirit). This confirms that the Holy Spirit is absolutely necessary for the working of miracles and financial provision
- In those days it was considered to be an insult for a Jewish host to fail in adequately providing wine for his guest
- The wine runs out (this could have been due to the oversight of how much the tally would be for the wedding and could not provide more)! This was disastrous for the hosts of the wedding! Mary approaches Jesus about the matter and He rebukes her, telling her that His time had not yet come—Remember that Jesus was in perfect tune to his Father's will. Perhaps Jesus was alluding to the fact that there was going to be a Wedding Feast at which He would be the Groom!
- Please understand that this was Cana of Galilee, which was a remote village far from the thriving city of Jerusalem. It was a dot on the map, without much for commerce, a nondescript village about 75 miles NW of Jerusalem—quite a huge distance in those days.
- This was not a major crisis—No one was starving, thirsty, destitute or any such thing. Hear me this was wine running out at a festive wedding where running out of wine was catastrophic as per their customs! This feat at the hands of Jesus is so incredible and it should serve to let us know and realize the following: the AWESOME nature of the God whom we serve; He is actively involved in every detail of our lives, even the minute and seemingly trivial...

- Another dimension of Father's heart is revealed in this all important First Miracle of Jesus—Everyone that was at that wedding feast benefited from that miracle – regardless of their personal state. Everyone benefited regardless of their level of need or lack or status in life.
- Everyone that was present benefited because of Jesus' relationship to the Father. It is exactly the same today—we all receive grace and mercy because of the righteousness of Christ!
- This is the all-important key in receiving from the Lord. It is because of the finished work of Calvary, and it has nothing to do with us trying to keep or fulfill a set of requirements!

FOUR VERY IMPORTANT FACTS TO CONSIDER—JOHN 2:11

This beginning of signs Jesus did in Cana of Galilee, and manifested His glory; and His disciples believed in Him.

1. The Law of first mention—This is the very first miracle and it was not done to meet the basic needs of people. This reveals Father's willingness to bless us materially way beyond our basic needs of water, food, clothing and shelter. In light of this first miracle this logic presents itself very strongly—If Christ reveals that Father is willing to provide naturally and financially in situations where no great need is present, then how much more in situations where great need is present!
2. This miracle was a sign—this sign was pointing to the fact that God had made provision for all men in Christ and that would be demonstrated in Him purchasing our redemption with His Blood!
3. This miracle manifested the glory of Christ. You have to understand this powerful significance. You see in the Jewish culture—Teachers (Rabbis) and disciples were not uncommon or unusual, so Jesus having disciples and being addressed as Teacher or Rabbi, was no big deal and did not automatically qualify Him to be the Messiah. So this miracle revealed His glory as truly The Anointed One—Glory Hallelujah!!!
4. This miracle caused His disciples to believe in Him. This is awesome as this is still relevant today. Obviously, they were following Him but

had not truly believed that He was the Messiah YET! It is quite evident that the training the disciples received was not just on an intellectual level. It also included the experience of miracles of provision.

SECOND MIRACLE OF PROVISION
The Feeding of The Five Thousand

Matthew 14:13-21

When Jesus heard it, He departed from there by boat to a deserted place by Himself. But when the multitudes heard it, they followed Him on foot from the cities. And when Jesus went out He saw a great multitude; and He was moved with compassion for them, and healed their sick. When it was evening, His disciples came to Him, saying, "This is a deserted place, and the hour is already late. Send the multitudes away, that they may go into the villages and buy themselves food." But Jesus said to them, "They do not need to go away. You give them something to eat." And they said to Him, "We have here only five loaves and two fish." He said, "Bring them here to Me." Then He commanded the multitudes to sit down on the grass. And He took the five loaves and the two fish, and looking up to heaven, He blessed and broke and gave the loaves to the disciples; and the disciples gave to the multitudes. So they all ate and were filled, and they took up twelve baskets full of the fragments that remained. Now those who had eaten were about five thousand men, besides women and children. (NKJV)

John the Baptist was killed, and Jesus wanted to be alone for a while. We are not sure as to the reason, if He wanted to reflect, to assess the timing in His own life, knowing that the reason why He came was to die.

In any event the multitudes followed Him. A valuable point to note here:

- He took a boat ride into a deserted place, and when they heard of it, they left their cities and followed Him. "Followed Him on foot from the cities"–This implies a great journey, effort, determination, the expending of energy.

This I believe was the foundation for this incredible miracle of resource provision to be done.

The Bible said that when Jesus saw the multitude He was moved with compassion and began to heal them. I tell you that a lot of times Jesus will be moved with compassion when He sees our determined press towards Him—Faith without works is dead. The woman with the issue of blood readily comes to mind. She had spent everything she had on doctors and charlatans to be cured. She literally crawled through a crowd to barely touch the hem of Jesus' garment. That is a great cost to her. She was so weak and she persevered. See Matthew 9:20-22.

Hear me, these people did not consider the extent of the price to be paid, they journeyed for a considerable distance and did not pack any food to eat or mats to sleep on, maybe not even an extra cloak. All they wanted was to see Jesus. Sometimes it can be the same for us when we are called to give up our basic needs to meet Him in the greater purpose He has for us.

It was getting late and the stomachs of the disciples were likely growling. They decided to tell Jesus it was time for the meeting to be over. "This service went on far too long, we are sure that the people are hungry because we are. Send them away so that they can provide for themselves." Even the disciples were some of the most clueless people when God is about to work an impossible feat for His glory.

I tell you a lot of times when the Lord is about to move in an incredible way, we begin to look at natural circumstances—"well we do not have this, and we do not have that" we say!

Christ was in a different zone and challenged the disciples to give the people something to eat rather than sending them away. However, they had already assessed the situation and realized that all they had was five loaves and two fish.

Oh!!! I tell you some of the most powerful and creative miracles of financial provision begin with what we have to give to the Lord. In this particular case they could have concluded that this was of no use in the light of the vast multitude and could have told the young boy to eat his meal.

Another interesting point to note here—at times the sacrifice we make by giving what we have to the Lord can open up the door for great financial blessings for others. Come on, only this young man had food that day. If Jesus wanted, He could have called food down from heaven.

Remember how the Manna fell daily and miraculously for the Israelites, didn't it? But He wants us to be co-labourers in these kinds of miracles.

The next thing that He does is to instruct the disciples to have the people sit–(come to a place of rest) ... To enter into those secret dimensions of hidden provision we all have to come to the PLACE OF REST!

He then Blesses and Breaks and wow, provision was made–the multitude of over five thousand people was fed on five loaves and two fishes. That's all we need at times BLESS AND Break and ABUNDANCE will FLOW!!!—Next thing we know 12 Baskets of "leftovers" are collected–one for each disciple and his family and any who might have been famished!!!

Incredible lesson of supernatural provision, and as such we should never be afraid of serving others first, knowing that in the Kingdom there will always be more than enough for everyone. God will meet our needs and that of our families.

Remember—SACRIFICE releases SUPERNATURAL SUPPLIES—We do not have to be bound by this world's financial system that is based on lack and competition for that lack.

You see it should have been easy for them to believe that Jesus could have provided for their basic needs, after all He just healed the multitude of all kinds of sickness and diseases. A lot of times we can believe the Lord to heal and meet other peoples' needs but have problems believing for our own needs.

THIRD MIRACLE OF FINANCIAL PROVISION
Feeding Of the Four Thousand—Matthew 15:29-39

> *Jesus departed from there, skirted the Sea of Galilee, and went up on the mountain and sat down there. Then great multitudes came to Him, having with them the lame, blind, mute, maimed, and many others; and they laid them down at Jesus' feet, and He healed them. So the multitude marveled when they saw the mute speaking, the* [b] *maimed made whole, the lame walking, and the blind seeing; and they glorified the God of Israel. Now Jesus called His disciples to Himself and said, "I have compassion on the multitude, because they have now continued with Me three days and have nothing to eat. And I do not want to send them away hungry, lest they faint on the way." Then His disciples said to Him, "Where could we get*

enough bread in the wilderness to fill such a great multitude?" Jesus said to them, "How many loaves do you have?" And they said, "Seven, and a few little fish." So He commanded the multitude to sit down on the ground. And He took the seven loaves and the fish and gave thanks, broke them and gave them to His disciples; and the disciples gave to the multitude. So they all ate and were filled, and they took up seven large baskets full of the fragments that were left. Now those who ate were four thousand men, besides women and children. And He sent away the multitude, got into the boat, and came to the region of Magdala.

This time the situation was very similar to the previous feeding of the five thousand but with some very pertinent added information or dimensions.

This time we learn that the people had spent three full days without food; totally engrossed and involved in what was taking place.

We also learn unlike the first time when the duration of time was considerably less and twelve baskets of leftovers were collected, this time they were three days and only seven baskets of leftovers collected.

I believe that Jesus was teaching His disciples an important lesson on the value of Community and Sharing—For three days no one moved... From the very first person that got their healing or deliverance on the first day to the last person that got theirs on the third day. That was AWESOME and showed the power and value of COMMUNITY!!!

Unlike the first miracle when 12 Baskets were collected, and each Disciple got one this time they had to divide the 7 baskets among themselves. VERY POWERFUL STUFF!!!

FOURTH MIRACLE OF FINANCIAL PROVISION
Provision To Pay Taxes:

Matthew 17:24-27

When they had come to Capernaum, those who received the temple tax came to Peter and said, "Does your Teacher not pay the temple tax?" He said, "Yes." And when he had come into the house, Jesus anticipated him, saying, "What do you think, Simon? From whom do

> the kings of the earth take customs or taxes, from their sons or from strangers?" Peter said to Him, "From strangers." Jesus said to him, "Then the sons are free. Nevertheless, lest we offend them, go to the sea, cast in a hook, and take the fish that comes up first. And when you have opened its mouth, you will find a piece of money; take that and give it to them for Me and you."

This was not a tax to be paid to the Roman government of the day, but it was to be paid to the Jewish officials for the upkeep of the Temple. This had nothing to do with their usual tithes and/or offerings, this was instituted by Moses in Exodus 30:13-16 and was used for the upkeep of the then Tabernacle.

It was to be taken from every male over 20 years old and was to be taken anytime there was a census taken. This later became a way to raise money for the Temple and it was done annually.

The issue here was the demand placed on Jesus to pay the Temple tax to which He declared that as a Son of the House, He has no obligation to pay taxes. Again this had nothing to do with Tithes and Offerings, this was a separate tax and Jesus was right in what He stated.

It is like you owning a hotel and charging your children a tax for the upkeep, no you would charge your paying guests for that.

In any event Jesus then instructed Peter to catch a fish and in that fish's mouth he found the necessary money to pay the tax. This was done so that no offence would come.

Very interesting thing to note here:

- This money did not come from their present resource
- There are times when Jesus would provide us with an extra source of resource to give when we are not obligated to do so, so that people do not become offended by our liberty.
- There is money hidden in the mouth of some fish (representing the unsaved). We need to know how to tap those realms at times. Not all our provision would come directly from the saved or church.

This brings us to a very important dynamic as we seek to uncover the secrets to hidden wealth: The dynamics of Solomon's technology of building.

LET'S CHECK OUR UNDERSTANDING OF CHAPTER 2:—JESUS' MIRACLES OF PROVISION.

John 2:1-11–The Wedding Feast at Cana
1. Who was present at this first miracle?
2. Do you agree the above scripture shows God the Father's approval of marriage? Explain.
3. What principles can we glean or understand from this miracle that Jesus performed in Cana of Galilee?
4. Why do you think that the bible was careful to mention that they (Jesus, His first disciples and Mary) were invited guests?

Matthew 14:13-21—The Feeding of The Five Thousand
1. What is signified by the fact that "they followed Him on foot from the cities"?
2. Why was this determination and effort to seek His presence important?
3. Based on the disciples urging Jesus to let the people go, can you identify a pattern between our own thinking and that of the disciples?
4. Can you identify some of the talent and resources that God has placed within your command that can be used for His purposes – towards the advancement of His Kingdom upon the earth?
5. **Fill in the blanks:**
   S_ _ _ _ _ _ _E releases S _ _ _ _N_ _ _ _ _ L S _ _ _ _ _ _ S. We _ _ not have to be b_ _ _d by this w_ _ _d's f_ _ _ _ _ _ _l system that is based on lack and c_ _ _ _ _ _ _ _ _n for that lack.

Matthew 15:29-39—Feeding of the Four Thousand
1. What were the significant differences between these 2 instances of feeding the crowds?
2. What is the important lesson that Jesus was trying to teach His disciples through this miracle?
3. Unlike the first miracle when _ _ B _ _ _ _ _s were collected, and each D_ _ _ _ _ _e got one, this time they had to d_ _ _ _e the S_ _ _n baskets among themselves.

Matthew 17: 24-27—Provision to Pay Taxes
1. What was the purpose of this Tax and to whom was it to be paid?
2. Why did Jesus take issue at the demand placed upon Him to pay this Tax?
3. For what reason did Jesus instruct Peter to take the money from the fish's mouth and pay the necessary taxes?
4. What are some of the important facts that we could glean from this miracle?

CHAPTER THREE
DYNAMICS OF SOLOMON'S TECHNOLOGY OF BUILDING

PARTNERSHIP WITH HIRAM:

2 Chronicles 2:1–18

Then Solomon determined to build a temple for the name of the Lord, and a royal house for himself. Solomon selected seventy thousand men to bear burdens, eighty thousand to quarry stone in the mountains, and three thousand six hundred to oversee them. Then Solomon sent to Hiram king of Tyre, saying: As you have dealt with David my father, and sent him cedars to build himself a house to dwell in, so deal with me. Behold, I am building a temple for the name of the Lord my God, to dedicate it to Him, to burn before Him [b]sweet incense, for the continual showbread, for the burnt offerings morning and evening, on the Sabbaths, on the New Moons, and on the [c]set feasts of the Lord our God. This is an ordinance forever to Israel. And the temple which I build will be great, for our God is greater than all gods. But who is able to build Him a temple, since heaven and the heaven of heavens cannot contain Him? Who am I then, that I should build Him a temple, except to burn sacrifice before Him? Therefore send me at once a man skillful to work in gold and silver, in bronze and iron, in purple and crimson and blue, who has skill to engrave with the skillful men who are with me in Judah and Jerusalem, whom David my father provided. Also send me cedar and cypress and algum logs from Lebanon, for I know that your servants have skill to cut timber in Lebanon; and indeed my servants will be with your servants, to prepare timber for me in abundance, for the temple which I am about to build shall be great and wonderful. And indeed I will give to your servants, the woodsmen who cut timber, twenty thousand kors of ground wheat, twenty thousand kors of barley, twenty thousand baths of wine, and twenty thousand baths of oil. Then Hiram king of Tyre answered in writing, which he sent to Solomon: Because the LORD loves His people, He has made you king over them. Hiram also said: Blessed be the LORD God of Israel, who made heaven and earth, for He has given King David a wise son, endowed with prudence and understanding, who will build a temple for the LORD and a royal house for himself! And now I have sent a skillful man, endowed with understanding, Huram my master craftsman (the son of a woman of the daughters of Dan, and his father was a man of Tyre), skilled to work in gold and silver, bronze and iron, stone and wood, purple and blue, fine linen and crimson, and to make any engraving and to accomplish any plan which may be given to him, with your skillful men and with the skillful men of my lord David your father. Now therefore, the wheat, the barley, the oil, and the wine which my lord has spoken of, let him send to his servants. And we will cut wood from Lebanon, as much as you need; we will bring it to you in rafts by sea to Joppa, and you will carry it up to Jerusalem. Then Solomon numbered all the aliens who were in the land of Israel, after the census in which David his father had numbered them; and there were found to be one hundred and fifty-three thousand six hundred. And he made seventy thousand of them bearers of burdens, eighty thousand stonecutters in the mountain, and three thousand six hundred overseers to make the people work.

THE EXTENSION OF THE BUILDING PROCESS INTO PARTNERSHIP WITH THE RE-sources of the world system—Please note the following:

- Both David and Solomon partnered with Hiram.
- Hiram had built a house for David (2 Samuel 5:11).

Chapter Three: Dynamics of Solomon's Technology of Building

- Hiram is the king of Tyre:
- Note Tyre is a type of satan and the world system: Ezekiel 28 (proclamation against the Prince and King of Tyre.
- Tyre represents the economic commercial system of the world. It has the capacity to gain wealth, trade and operates out of the wisdom of the world in gaining riches.

Ezekiel 28:12-13, states (You were in Eden, the garden of God; every precious stone was your covering: the sardius, topaz, and diamond, Beryl, onyx, and jasper, sapphire, turquoise, and emerald with gold. The workmanship of your timbrels and pipes was prepared for you on the day you were created.) It is made clear that the King of Tyre is satan and the prince of Tyre is the economic system of the earth.

We are called to be the salt of the earth. We have to find the technology by which we can invade the systems of the earth, partnership with Hiram, and take resources out of the world to build the house of God.

That's the technology of Solomon, the technology to build a glorious house by extracting from the world that which we need. Solomon therefore utilises the wealth and the resources, knowledge, skill of the world system to enrich his kingdom. We are in the world but not of the world. We are not making covenant with the spirit of the world, but we will interact with and use the systems and technology of the world to build for God.

Note also that Moses' Tabernacle was built with Egyptian wealth.

MORE WISDOM TO GAIN WEALTH FROM KING SOLOMON:

1 Kings 9:26–28

King Solomon also built a fleet of ships at Ezion Geber, which is near Elath on the shore of the Red Sea, in the land of Edom. Then Hiram sent his servants with the fleet, seamen who knew the sea, to work with the servants of Solomon. And they went to Ophir, and acquired four hundred and twenty talents of gold from there, and brought it to King Solomon.

1 Kings 10:21-23

All King Solomon's drinking vessels were gold, and all the vessels of the House of the Forest of Lebanon were pure gold. Not one was silver, for this was accounted as nothing in the days of Solomon. For the king had merchant ships at sea with the fleet of Hiram. Once every three years the merchant ships came bringing gold, silver, ivory, apes, and monkeys. So King Solomon surpassed all the kings of the earth in riches and wisdom.

For Solomon, building the House of God involved getting into the ship building business. Not in Jerusalem, but in Edom, with activities extending all the way to Ophir. Yet all of this was temple building. This answers those who question what right "businesses" have involving themselves in "church" activity. The business is about church, and church is about business—Kingdom Business.

PARABLE OF JESUS:

Luke 16:1-14

He also said to His disciples: "There was a certain rich man who had a steward, and an accusation was brought to him that this man was wasting his goods. So he called him and said to him, 'What is this I hear about you? Give an account of your stewardship, for you can no longer be steward.' "Then the steward said within himself, 'What shall I do? For my master is taking the stewardship away from me. I cannot dig; I am ashamed to beg. I have resolved what to do, that when I am put out of the stewardship, they may receive me into their houses.' "So he called every one of his master's debtors to him, and said to the first, 'How much do you owe my master?' And he said, 'A hundred measures of oil.' So he said to him, 'Take your bill, and sit down quickly and write fifty.' Then he said to another, 'And how much do you owe?' So he said, 'A hundred measures of wheat.' And he said to him, 'Take your bill, and write eighty.' So the master commended the unjust steward because he had dealt shrewdly. For the sons of this world are more shrewd in their generation than the sons of light. "And I say to you, make friends for yourselves by unrighteous [d]mammon, that when you fail, they may receive you into an everlasting home. He who is faithful in what is least is faithful also in much; and he who is unjust in what is least is unjust also in much. Therefore if you have not been faithful in the unrighteous mammon, who will commit to your trust the true riches? And if you have not been faithful in what is another man's, who will give you what is your own? "No servant can serve two masters; for either he will hate the one and love the other, or else he will be loyal to the one and despise the other. You cannot serve God and mammon." Now the Pharisees, who were lovers of money, also heard all these things, and they derided Him.

A Pharisee spirit cannot accept this mentality 'to be shrewd in your generation'

Jesus is not advocating dishonesty, but he is proposing effective interaction with the world system for material advance. Shrewd in this context means sensible right action in the midst of the real world, material situations.

The Apostolic is associated with principles of gathering and distribution Acts 4:33–37

And with great power the apostles gave witness to the resurrection of the Lord Jesus. And great grace was upon them all. Nor was there anyone among them who lacked; for all who were possessors of lands or houses sold them, and brought the proceeds of the things that were sold, and laid them at the apostles' feet; and they distributed to each as anyone had need. And Joses, who was also named Barnabas by the apostles (which is translated Son of Encouragement), a Levite of the country of Cyprus, having land, sold it, and brought the money and laid it at the apostles' feet.

Genesis 41:44, 48–49, 55–56

Pharaoh also said to Joseph, "I am Pharaoh, and without your consent no man may lift his hand or foot in all the land of Egypt."

So he gathered up all the food of the seven years which were in the land of Egypt, and laid up the food in the cities; he laid up in every city the food of the fields which surrounded them. Joseph gathered very much grain, as the sand of the sea, until he stopped counting, for it was immeasurable.

So when all the land of Egypt was famished, the people cried to Pharaoh for bread. Then Pharaoh said to all the Egyptians, "Go to Joseph; whatever he says to you, do." The famine was over all the face of the earth, and Joseph opened all the storehouses and sold to the Egyptians. And the famine became severe in the land of Egypt.

This is a Joseph principle. The apostolic dimension deals with economic issues.

Before proceeding further I would like to ensure a critical balance to acquisition of wealth and finances as I do not want any of us to lose our focus and make the acquisition of wealth our primary focus instead of the Lord and knowing Him fully and wholly as Redeemer, Wonderful, Counsellor, Everlasting Father, Prince of Peace and the Lover of our souls.

LET'S CHECK OUR UNDERSTANDING OF CHAPTER 3:—DYNAMICS OF SOLOMON'S TECHNOLOGY OF BUILDING.

1. Who was Hiram and what were his interactions with the Kings of Israel?
2. According to Ezekiel 28, what does Tyre represent?
3. Who does Ezekiel liken the Prince of Tyre to?
4. Why is it so interesting and yet controversial that both King David and King Solomon should partner with Hiram the King of Tyre?
5. What is the technology of Solomon?
6. Where did the resources/wealth for building of the Tabernacle during Moses' time come from?
7. The author says "This answers the question what right "business" have involving themselves in "Church" activity. The business is about Church, and Church is about business—Kingdom Business." Do you agree? Why or Why not?
8. What was the reason for the Pharisees to deride Jesus?

9. How does Jesus suggest we be shrewd in our own generation just like Solomon in his?
10. What does the Apostolic function deal with? Acts 4:33-37; Genesis 41:44, 48-49, 55-56

CHAPTER FOUR
THE ISSUE OF CONTENTMENT

PAUL'S ADMONITION TO TIMOTHY

1 Timothy 6:5-10

Eventually there's an epidemic of backstabbing, and truth is but a distant memory. They think religion is a way to make a fast buck. A devout life does bring wealth, but it's the rich simplicity of being yourself before God. Since we entered the world penniless and will leave it penniless, if we have bread on the table and shoes on our feet, that's enough. But if it's only money these leaders are after, they'll self-destruct in no time. Lust for money brings trouble and nothing but trouble. Going down that path, some lose their footing in the faith completely and live to regret it bitterly ever after. MSG

...and constant friction between men of corrupt mind, who have been robbed of the truth and who think that godliness is a means to financial gain. But godliness with contentment is great gain. For we brought nothing into the world, and we can take nothing out of it. But if we have food and clothing, we will be content with that. People who want to get rich fall into temptation and a trap and into many foolish and harmful desires that plunge men into ruin and destruction. For the love of money is a root of all kinds of evil.

Some people, eager for money, have wandered from the faith and pierced themselves with many griefs. NIV

PLEASE UNDERSTAND THE CONTEXT HERE: IT HAD TO DO WITH WORK AND HOW to conduct oneself and it was from that premise that the Apostle Paul released this powerful revelation.

The emphasis cannot be money but a correct heart position. It is an established fact that the Lord desires to bless us financially.

GODLINESS AS A MEANS OF FINANCIAL GAIN!!!

The Apostle makes it quite clear that anyone who teaches Godliness as a means to gain wealth and prosperity has a depraved mind—1 Timothy 6:5

DEPRAVED—is often translated Corrupt or Decaying and comes from the Greek word "diapheheiro" and is used in reference to **the damage a moth does to cloth**.

There is also another Greek word used, "apostereo" which means; to be robbed of the truth through the corrupt condition of the mind. In this case false doctrines have corrupted or robbed the mind into thinking that Godliness is a means to gain and wealth.

However, the Apostle also added a very important ingredient and made it abundantly clear that Godliness will produce great gain when Contentment rules the heart.

GODLINESS in the verse is a very interesting Greek word. It is the word EUSEBEIA, which comes from two words:

EU—Good or Well
SEBOMAI—To be Devout

It means unequivocally that Godliness is the Behaviour that is the outcome of the desire to please God. For this reason, it is of the utmost importance that we do not primarily seek MONEY or RICHES from the Lord, but rather seek to have a DESIRE TO PLEASE HIM and let HIM release the favour and wisdom for us to gain wealth.

Hear me Today—A Godly FOCUS will produce CONTENTMENT and GREAT PEACE. A material focus will produce anxiety, fear and greed.

Also, remember, seeking security in riches will not prepare us to face the righteous judgement that is to come—1 Timothy 6:7-8

For we brought nothing into this world, and it is certain we can carry nothing out. And having food and clothing, with these we shall be content.

LET'S CHECK OUR UNDERSTANDING OF CHAPTER 4—THE ISSUE OF CONTENTMENT.

1. The author commenting on 1Timothy 6:5-10 says "It had to do with work and how to conduct oneself and it was from that premise that the Apostle Paul released this powerful revelation. The emphasis cannot be money, but a correct hear position." Do you agree with this position? Explain.
2. What is meant by a "depraved" mind in 1 Timothy 6:5?
3. What is the Greek word translated Godliness in 1 Timothy 6:5? What are it's roots?
4. Why did the Apostle add this very important ingredient/word in debunking the prevalent teaching that "godliness is a means of gain"?
5. How will developing a "Godly FOCUS" positively affect us?
6. Fill in the Blanks:
7. For we b_ _ _ _ _ _ nothing into this w_ _ _ _, and it is c_ _ _ _ _ _ we can c_ _ _ _ nothing out. And having _ _ _ _ and _ _ _ _ _ _ _ _, with these we shall be _ _ _ _ _ _ _

CHAPTER FIVE
THE DESIRE TO BE RICH

1 Timothy 6:9

But those who desire to be rich fall into temptation and a snare, and into many foolish and harmful lusts which drown men in destruction and perdition.

THE ACQUISITION OF WEALTH MUST BE A BY-PRODUCT OF DESIRING TO PLEASE God and doing of His Will. It must never be about desiring to be wealthy in order to please the Lord and do His Will. That is a backfiring slippery slope which the believer should never desire!

THE DESIRE TO BE RICH PRODUCES THREE THINGS:

1. It leads to FALLING INTO TEMPTATIONS. Remember, ***it is the focus of a life that determines its experience.*** In other words, when our motivation is incorrect then other things will get seriously out of kilter. Temptations will become more difficult to resist.
2. It leads to a SNARE—a device for trapping birds and animals. It is an experience or thing that may appear alluring and attractive but it entangles the unwary. In essence it is a trap. Drugs, illicit affiliations, cheating a little here and there might appear attractive now that we have "made it" and moved into the echelons of the rich and

richer. Without Jesus as the rudder, the longing of the heart of avarice, will lead to destruction for anybody entangled in that path. They are snared!
3. It leads to MANY FOOLISH AND HARMFUL DESIRES which plunge men into ruin and destruction.

Foolish in Greek is the word "*ANOETOS*" and it literally means "**WITHOUT MIND**". It means to do things without thinking, without applying reasoned thought.

Harmful on the other hand comes from the Greek word "DABEROS" which means to cause injury or to do damage to someone.

Ruin and Destruction—"OLETHROS"—physical ruin or destruction of one's well-being. Your emotional state becomes messed-up.

LOVE OF MONEY

The love of and not money in and of itself is the root of all evil. This phrase "the love of money" comes from one single Greek word—"PHILARGUROS" which is a compounded word, the first part being:

PHILO—meaning LOVE and the second being ARGUROS—meaning SILVER. So it literally means: "One who loves silver". This word is also sometimes used to translate covetous.

THE ROOT OF ALL EVIL

In the original Greek it says ***A root of all the evils***. The Greek word for root is the word "rhiza" and it is used to describe the root of a plant. It gives the picture of a root growing deep into a person's life. This root is hidden from sight, from others and even from us.

This root produces an evil tree that produces all kinds of evil fruit that may seem unrelated. However, the Apostle Paul was revealing that the love of money will nourish all the evils that plague society. He is not saying that the love of money is the only root that produces evil fruit; he simply means that it can produce evil of all varieties.

Next, we will explore the Rich Young Ruler's encounter with Christ to see what can be learnt from that encounter.

LET'S CHECK OUR UNDERSTANDING OF CHAPTER 5—THE DESIRE TO BE RICH.

1. Fill in the Blanks.
The a_____n of w___h must be a by-product of d_____g to please G__ and doing of His W___. It must never be about d_____g to be w____y in order to p____e the Lord and do His Will. That is a backfiring s_____y s___e which the b_____r should never d____e!

2. What are the 3 undesirable by-products resulting from a desire to be rich?

3. What is the Greek word translated Foolish in 1 Timothy 6:9 and what does it mean?

4. The author says, "the love of money and not money in and of itself is the root of all evil." Do you agree? Explain with Scriptural references.

5. The Greek word "PHILARGUROS" made up of P____ - meaning L___ and A_____ - meaning S_____, translated into English as Love of Money, literally means O__ who L____ S_____.

6. This same word Philarguros is sometimes also translated as C_____s.

7. Elaborate on the phrase "Root of All Evil."

8. Do you agree with Apostle Paul when he says in 1 Timothy 6:10 "For the Love of Money is a root of all kinds of evil, for which some have strayed from the faith in their greediness and pieced themselves through with many sorrows."?

CHAPTER SIX
THE RICH YOUNG RULER'S ENCOUNTER WITH CHRIST

AS A PRECURSOR TO THAT ENCOUNTER LET US BRIEFLY LOOK AT MATTHEW 13:44-46

> God's kingdom is like a treasure hidden in a field for years and then accidentally found by a trespasser. The finder is ecstatic—what a find!—and proceeds to sell everything he owns to raise money and buy that field. "Or God's kingdom is like a jewel merchant on the hunt for excellent pearls. Finding one that is flawless, he immediately sells everything and buys it. MSG

Both these parables speak to us about Total Commitment to Christ and The Kingdom. It speaks about the Willingness to Give Up All to get Him. Luke 14:33 declares:

> Simply put, if you're not willing to take what is dearest to you, whether plans or people, and kiss it good-bye, you can't be my disciple. MSG

> So then, every one of you who does not forsake all his possessions, he cannot be My disciple.

ANOTHER LOOK AT LUKE 14:25-27

Now great multitudes went with Him. And He turned and said to them, "If anyone comes to Me and does not hate his father and mother, wife and children, brothers and sisters, yes, and his own life also, he cannot be My disciple. And whoever does not bear his cross and come after Me cannot be My disciple.

- Please understand that in the First Century a cross was not a religious symbol as we make it today. The cross was an everyday occurrence—as a matter of fact it was one of the prescribed methods of execution, so it was a symbol of death.
- In essence Christ was calling His disciples and as such us also to a sacrificial, Christ-Centered Lifestyle. Take up your cross and follow Him to a similar death.

As we go into the parable of the Rich Young Ruler, we need to understand that this was not the case of *"impulsive giving"* or giving under some kind of pressure. This was an encounter with Jesus and what He spoke to this young man.

THE RICH YOUNG RULER

It is somewhat interesting to note that Matthew, Mark and Luke all record the encounter with Jesus and this man. However, none of them actually said that he was a Rich Young Ruler. This was deduced from reading all three accounts.

Matthew 19:16-22 describes him as a young man who was rich

Now behold, one came and said to Him, "Good Teacher, what good thing shall I do that I may have eternal life?" So He said to him, "Why do you call Me good? No one is good but One, that is, God. But if you want to enter into life, keep the commandments." He said to Him, "Which ones?" Jesus said, "'You shall not murder,' 'You shall not commit adultery,' 'You shall not steal,' 'You shall not bear false witness,' 'Honor your father and your mother,' and, 'You shall love your neighbor as yourself.' " The young man said to Him, "All these things I have kept from my youth. What do I still lack?" Jesus said to him, "If you want to be perfect, go, sell what you have and give to the poor, and you will have treasure in heaven; and come, follow Me." But when the young man heard that saying, he went away sorrowful, for he had great possessions.

Mark 10:17-30 describes him as one who came to Jesus and that he was rich

Now as He was going out on the road, one came running, knelt before Him, and asked Him, "Good Teacher, what shall I do that I may inherit eternal life?" So Jesus said to him, "Why do you call Me good? No one is good but One, that is, God. You know the commandments: 'Do not commit adultery,' 'Do not murder,' 'Do not steal,' 'Do not bear false witness,' 'Do not defraud,' 'Honor your father and your mother.' " And he answered and said to Him, "Teacher, all these things I have kept from my youth." Then Jesus, looking at him, loved him, and said to him, "One thing you lack: Go your way, sell whatever you have and give to the poor, and you will have treasure in heaven; and come, take up the cross, and follow Me." But he was sad at this word, and went away sorrowful, for he had great possessions. Then Jesus looked around and said to His disciples, "How hard it is for those who have riches to enter the kingdom of God!" And the disciples were astonished at His words. But Jesus answered again and said to them, "Children, how hard it is for those who trust in riches to enter the kingdom of God! It is easier for a camel to go through the eye of a needle than for a rich man to enter the kingdom of God." And they were greatly astonished, saying among themselves, "Who then can be saved?" But Jesus looked at them and said, "With men it is impossible, but not with God; for with God all things are possible." Then Peter began to say to Him, "See, we have left all and followed You." So Jesus answered and said, "Assuredly, I say to you, there is no one who has left house or brothers or sisters or father or mother or wife or children or lands, for My sake and the gospel's, who shall not receive a hundredfold now in this time—houses and brothers and sisters and mothers and children and lands, with persecutions— and in the age to come, eternal life.

Luke 18:18-30 describes him as a certain ruler who was rich

Now a certain ruler asked Him, saying, "Good Teacher, what shall I do to inherit eternal life?" So Jesus said to him, "Why do you call Me good? No one is good but One, that is, God. You know the commandments: 'Do not commit adultery,' 'Do not murder,' 'Do not steal,' 'Do not bear false witness,' 'Honor your father and your mother.'" And he said, "All these things I have kept from my youth." So when Jesus heard these things, He said to him, "You still lack one thing. Sell all that you have and distribute to the poor, and you will have treasure in heaven; and come, follow Me." But when he heard this, he became very sorrowful, for he was very rich. And when Jesus saw that he became very sorrowful, He said, "How hard it is for those who have riches to enter the kingdom of God! For it is easier for a camel to go through the eye of a needle than for a rich man to enter the kingdom of God." And those who heard it said, "Who then can be saved?" But He said, "The things which are impossible with men are possible with God." Then Peter said, "See, we have left all and followed You." So He said to them, "Assuredly, I say to you, there is no one who has left house or parents or brothers or wife or children, for the sake of the kingdom of God, who shall not receive many times more in this present time, and in the age to come eternal life."

Hence the designation—"The Rich Young Ruler"

The one common thread that we have running through all three accounts is that he was rich. Now, some may say well this parable does not apply to me because I am not rich. However, as we will see later on from Peter's question it applies to all of us.

Our study will center in the account given by Matthew 19:16-22

Now behold, one came and said to Him, "Good Teacher, <u>what good thing shall I do that I may have eternal life?</u>" So He said to him, "Why do you call Me good? No one is good but One, that is, God. But if you want to enter into life, keep the commandments." He said to Him, "<u>Which ones?</u>" Jesus said, "'You shall not murder,' 'You shall not commit adultery,' 'You shall not steal,' 'You shall not bear false witness,' 'Honor your father and your mother,' and, 'You shall love *your neighbor as yourself.' " The young man said to Him, "<u>All these things I have kept from my youth. What do I still lack?</u>" Jesus said to him, "If you want to be perfect, go, sell what you have and give to the poor, and you will have treasure in heaven; and come, follow Me." But when the young man heard that saying, he went away sorrowful, for he had great possessions. [Emphasis Author's]*

THREE IMPORTANT QUESTIONS

All three of the Rich Young Ruler's questions were centered on his lack of assurance about Eternal Life. It was very clear that he was dissatisfied with his religious experience and was seeking more.

QUESTION ONE—WHAT *GOOD THING* HE MUST *DO* TO OBTAIN ETERNAL LIFE

Christ's Response

Firstly He points the young man away from *Doing good things* to the fact that God is Good – making Good a person! He then goes on to tell him that the issue was not his good works but Faith in the Good One—God!

Christ also changed his focus from obtaining eternal life to entering into life. In essence He told him that he could not OWN or POSSESS Eternal Life because it belonged to God. He could only enter into life by having a relationship with its owner—GOD!

He also redirected his focus from something to be achieved later at one's death to the present reality of NOW! He then points him to the Law of Moses as a means of entering into life. This was not unexpected as he was a Jew living under the Law because Christ had not yet died.

This prompted the Rich Young Ruler towards the obvious:

QUESTION TWO—WHICH COMMANDS NEED TO BE KEPT?

This was a very legitimate question as there were hundreds of commandments to be kept under Moses' Law. Of course this is the problem with the Law of Moses as the individual must keep some laws and ignore the others. There was just no way to perfectly keep the Law of Moses all the time so the question was legitimate.

Christ's Response
You shall not murder, you shall not commit adultery, you shall not steal, you shall not bear false witness, honour your father and mother, and you shall love your neighbour as yourself, (this one seems to modify the commandment—you shall not covet).

Interesting though is the fact that Jesus only identified these six as they all had to do with horizontal relationships—relationship between fellow human beings. The other four commandments deal with our vertical relationship—our relationship with God.

Jesus purposely left out these four commandments for a very important reason. Please understand that this young man was a Jew and as such knew the Law.

Jesus wanted to deal with the real issue in his life (the love of his wealth) and draw the obvious parallel to it. He was seeking to deal with the young man's relationship to God in regard to his wealth.

No doubt the Rich Young Ruler thought that Jesus would address his relationship to God through his next question:

QUESTION THREE—I HAVE DONE ALL SIX OF THESE COMMANDMENTS—WHAT AM I STILL LACKING?

Keeping the Law of Moses had not liberated this young man. In fact the Law has revealed to him that something was lacking—he had no life with God.

Christ had skilfully set the stage for this young man to hear what God required for him to enter into life.

Christ could have quoted the other four commandments—you shall not have any gods before me… you shall not make any graven images… you shall not take the Name of the Lord in vain and remember the Sabbath day…

The commands that Jesus did not preface during this conversation allowed Him to zero in on the main issue of the rich young ruler's life—his love of his wealth which had become a god in his life. He violated the commandment of not having any other god besides the true God in his life. No doubt he gave alms to the poor, but giving wholeheartedly is another thing!

Christ's Response—Sell all your possessions and give it to the poor and you shall have treasure in heaven, and come and follow Me.

Christ boils everything down to three specific commands for the Rich Young Ruler to enter into life:

- First, he must **Sell All** his possessions
- Second, he must ***give the money obtained from the sale*** to the poor
- Third, he must then follow Christ.

Please note a very interesting point—Jesus did not tell the Rich Young Ruler to give his possessions to the poor which would have been the easier thing to do. Instead He told him to sell what he had and then give the proceeds of that sale to the poor. This process was much harder and there had to be a reason for it.

One would imagine that had he followed through, every time he sold a possession his attachment to material possession would have died a bit at a time and at the end of the process he would have completely died to the love of money and would have then been able to follow Christ to the fullest.

However, we know the end; he could not break free from his love of money and material possessions. He was unable to enter into life because of his emotional attachment to temporal things; proving or revealing that money was his real god and that he was enslaved by it.

HARD FOR A RICH PERSON TO ENTER THE KINGDOM

The Rich Young Ruler's inability or unwillingness to obey Christ and **SELL ALL** to follow Him prompted Jesus to reveal to His disciples how difficult it was for these kinds of people to enter the Kingdom.

CAMEL THROUGH THE EYE OF A NEEDLE—MATTHEW 19:23-30

Then Jesus said to His disciples, "Assuredly, I say to you that it is hard for a rich man to enter the kingdom of heaven. And again I say to you, it is easier for a camel to go through the eye of a needle than for a rich man to enter the kingdom of God." When His disciples heard it, they were greatly astonished, saying, "Who then can be saved?" But Jesus looked at them and said to them, "With men this is impossible, but with God all things are possible." Then Peter answered and said to Him, "See, we have left all and followed You.

Therefore what shall we have?" So Jesus said to them, "Assuredly I say to you, that in the regeneration, when the Son of Man sits on the throne of His glory, you who have followed Me will also sit on twelve thrones, judging the twelve tribes of Israel. And everyone who has left houses or brothers or sisters or father or mother or wife or children or lands, for My name's sake, shall receive a hundredfold, and inherit eternal life. But many who are first will be last, and the last first.

This is what is known as an IDIOM—which is the language that is peculiar to a people or community. However, at times if it is used outside of that particular culture, it does not make any sense and must be explained. This is the case here in North America as we have never had camels as a mode of transportation.

For those listening to Jesus at that time understood the sheer impossibility of the task. A literal camel simply put, will not go through the eye of a needle.

In Jesus' time, the eye of a needle was a smaller gate set within a larger one as the cities were protected by having walls built around them. The sentries were posted to watch for attackers and marauders. The large gates were guarded and closed. This smaller gate was designed so that people could enter and exit the city without having to open the much larger gate. The larger gate in this case would have been used to allow the camel to pass through.

The imagery here is one of a camel fully laden with goods that could not bend down low enough to squeeze through the eye of the needle. What would have to happen is that the camel would have to be stripped of all its goods, get down on all fours and then stuffed forcibly through the gate.

This was a picture of the Rich Young Ruler having to offload all his possessions and then humbling himself (kneeling represents a sign of humility) in order to enter through the narrow gate leading into the Kingdom! Awesome!

You see, Jesus was correcting an incorrect belief system back then in the Jewish culture, which was—that rich men must be righteous, or God would not bless them with riches.

So here comes Jesus rocking the boat – not just rocking but capsizing it. The Jew obviously must have bought into that erroneous teaching and came to Jesus in a self-righteous state. And Jesus ripped through the religious assumption that his wealth was not a symbol of his righteous lifestyle, as a matter of fact the love for his wealth was an obstacle to his pleasing God.

This was a shocking new revelation even to Jesus' disciples; after all they also had a Jewish background. This prompted the surprised question from His disciples—**Who then Can Be Saved?**

JESUS ANSWERED—TO YOU THIS MAY SEEM IMPOSSIBLE, BUT NOT TO GOD!

Peter retorted with a very important statement of fact followed by a pertinent question!

He sees the implications of what Jesus was saying and brought up the fact that they did what the Rich Young Ruler could and did not do—Matthew 19:27

Jesus gives Peter and the other disciples a very straight and direct answer—no parable—to the pinpoint answer!—Matthew 19:28-29

In the first part of His answer Jesus reveals to them that there is a dimension of reward that will not be experienced or realized until the end of the age. Prompting us to understand that there are some things of a financial nature that we may sacrifice that we will not see immediate reward for—Hence the reason we cannot do these things from the premise seeking financial returns but from the premise of advancing the Kingdom in the earth!

He then goes on to reveal to them the promise of blessing and increase but only for those who LEAVE ALL to follow Him. This promise was not only for the twelve but for ANYONE who qualifies by LEAVING ALL for Him.

MATTHEW 19:29

In the original manuscripts the word wife was not included; it was later added by translators as they thought it would make for better reading. The NIV gives the clearest or closet translation of the original manuscript:

And everyone who has left houses or brothers or sisters or father or mother or children or fields for my sake will receive a hundred times as much and will inherit eternal life.

In some Bibles the word *wife* is in Italics meaning that it was added in by the translator and was not in the original text. And please don't use this as a reason to abandon your family!!!

Please note that this promise is for those who LEAVE ALL to follow Jesus and not for those who are willing in their hearts to leave all. As a matter-of-fact Matthew's account does not reveal the full context of Christ's message and as such, we should read it from Mark's account: **Mark 10:29-30**

However please understand that this verse is not to be taken out of context as some have and used it to claim 100-fold return on their giving. And then when it doesn't come back financially at 100-fold, the disenchanted, undisciplined new believer falls away. This is only to be used in the context of having LEFT ALL to follow Jesus and further His Kingdom in the earth.

FINAL THOUGHTS ON THIS ENCOUNTER BETWEEN THE RICH YOUNG RULER AND JESUS:

As we take a closer look at the accounts in Matthew, Mark and Luke we realize that there are some minor differences that reveal a wealth of interesting information, however all three of them record the fact that Jesus asked the Rich Young Ruler to SELL ALL his possessions and give the proceeds to the poor and he will have treasure in heaven and come and follow Him. Never did Jesus reveal the fact that there would have been blessings and rewards for him here on earth. Jesus wanted to make sure that his focus was right. Later on He revealed it to His disciples because they had already LEFT ALL to follow Him.

Mark's account records that they LEFT ALL for the Cause of Christ and the Gospel.

Luke's account records that they LEFT ALL for the Kingdom

However, one thing is duly noted that there was the motivation of reward. This is a very powerful principle in the Kingdom of God—MOTIVATION OF REWARD!

Having said that, we need to understand though because it is such a powerful principle we must be motivated accurately, or we could become very disillusioned and disappointed when we do not receive what we anticipated.

In all accounts they did not SELL ALL or LEAVE ALL so that they could get the 100-fold increase. The true disciple of Christ does it on the command of Jesus and entrusts his life to Him. The true disciple is not motivated to SELL or LEAVE ALL because of a desire to gain Wealth, Position or Prestige—Remember 1 Corinthians 13:3 and Mark 8:34-37

> *And though I bestow all my goods to feed the poor, and though I give my body to be burned, but have not love, it profits me nothing.*
> *When He had called the people to Himself, with His disciples also, He said to them, "Whoever desires to come after Me, let him deny himself, and take up his cross, and follow Me. For whoever desires to save his life will lose it, but whoever loses his life for My sake and the gospel's will save it. For what will it profit a man if he gains the whole world, and loses his own soul? Or what will a man give in exchange for his soul?*

Jesus then makes a statement that seems to be totally unrelated from the context; and only Matthew picks it up—In verse 30 Jesus declares "However, many who are first will be last, and many who are last will be first."

This had to do with what He was about to teach them and once again it had to deal with money. Very interesting to note that the majority of Jesus' parables were about money or wealth of some sort.

But before we go into the Parable of The Vineyard where Jesus reveals the dynamics of the first being last and the last being first let us explore the Parable of The Ten Minas:

The next parable on money that I want us to look at is, the Parable of the Ten Minas.

LET'S CHECK OUR UNDERSTANDING OF CHAPTER 6—THE RICH YOUNG RULER'S ENCOUNTER WITH CHRIST.

1. What did you understand from reading Matthew 13:44-46?
2. The author says: "both these parables (Matthew 13:44-46) speaks about total commitment to Christ and The Kingdom" Do you agree?

3. How will you describe the message from Luke 14:33?
4. For the First Century Christian what did the Cross symbolize?
5. What is the message to Christians from this passage of Scripture—Luke 14:25-27?
6. Based on the parable of "The Rich Young Ruler", do you recognize a focal point from which his three questions emerged?
7. What stands out to you in Jesus's response to this young ruler?
8. Do you agree with the author on the possible reason Jesus omitted 4 of the commandments that the rich young ruler should adhere to in-order to enter eternal life?
9. Fill in the Blanks:
Christ changed his focus from o _ _ _ _ _ _ _ g eternal life to e _ _ _ _ _ _ g into eternal life. In essence He told him that he could not O _ _ or P _ _ _ _ _ _ eternal life because it belonged to God. He could only e _ _ _ r eternal life by having a r _ _ _ _ _ _ _ _ _ _ p with its o _ _ _ r – G _ _. This is a re-direction of focus from something to be achieved l _ _ _ _ at one's death to the present reality of N _ _.
10. What seems to be blocking this Rich Young Ruler from entering eternal life? How did Jesus address this issue?
11. What did Jesus' disciples understand by the IDIOM He spoke in Matthew 19:23-30?
12. Which religious assumption was Jesus debunking through this IDIOM?
13. Just like the Rich Young Ruler, what are some of the things that we could be holding on to, that could hinder our capacity to enter eternal life?
14. Which portion of this IDIOM indicates the requirement for possessing humility to enter eternal life?
15. How did Jesus respond to the disciples' question of "Who then can be saved"?
16. Fill in the Blanks:
The promise of b _ _ _ _ _ _ g and i _ _ _ _ _ _ e but only for is only for those who L _ _ _ e a _ _ for Him. There are some things of a f _ _ _ _ _ _ _ l nature that we may s _ _ _ _ _ _ _ e that we may s _ _ _ _ _ _ _ e that we will not see i _ _ _ _ _ _ e reward. Hence we cannot do things from the premise s _ _ _ _ _ g financial r _ _ _ _ _ s but from the premise of a _ _ _ _ _ _ _ g the K _ _ _ _ _ m in the e _ _ _ _ h!

17. Contrast the difference between Matthew 19:29 and Mark 10:29-30.
18. Do you agree with the author on having to be careful in using this Scripture in the context it was meant as otherwise there is a great possibility of disenchanting Believers?
19. How will you explain Jesus' statement in Matthew 19:30 "However, many who are first will be last, and many who are last will be first."
20. What is your understanding of 1 Corinthians 13:3 and Mark 8:34-37?

CHAPTER SEVEN
THE PARABLE OF THE TEN MINAS

LUKE 19:11-26

Now as they heard these things, He spoke another parable, because He was near Jerusalem and because they thought the kingdom of God would appear immediately. Therefore He said: "A certain nobleman went into a far country to receive for himself a kingdom and to return. So he called ten of his servants, delivered to them ten minas, and said to them, 'Do business till I come.' But his citizens hated him, and sent a delegation after him, saying, 'We will not have this man to reign over us.' "And so it was that when he returned, having received the kingdom, he then commanded these servants, to whom he had given the money, to be called to him, that he might know how much every man had gained by trading. Then came the first, saying, 'Master, your mina has earned ten minas.' And he said to him, 'Well done, good servant; because you were faithful in a very little, have authority over ten cities.' And the second came, saying, 'Master, your mina has earned five minas.' Likewise, he said to him, 'You also be over five cities.' "Then another came, saying, 'Master, here is your mina, which I have kept put away in a handkerchief. For I feared you, because you are an austere man. You collect what you did not deposit, and reap what you did not sow.' And he said to him, 'Out of your own mouth I will judge you, you wicked servant.

You knew that I was an austere man, collecting what I did not deposit and reaping what I did not sow. Why then did you not put my money in the bank, that at my coming I might have collected it with interest?' "And he said to those who stood by, 'Take the mina from him, and give it to him who has ten minas.' (But they said to him, 'Master, he has ten minas.') 'For I say to you, that to everyone who has will be given; and from him who does not have, even what he has will be taken away from him.

THIS PARABLE IS RECORDED IN MATTHEW WITH SLIGHT DIFFERENCES, BUT IT carries the same meaning—Matthew 25:14-30

For the kingdom of heaven is like a man traveling to a far country, who called his own servants and delivered his goods to them. And to one he gave five talents, to another two, and to another one, to each according to his own ability; and immediately he went on a journey. Then he who had received the five talents went and traded with them, and made another five talents. And likewise he who had received two gained two more also. But he who had received one went and dug in the ground, and hid his lord's money. After a long time the lord of those servants came and settled accounts with them. "So he who had received five talents came and brought five other talents, saying, 'Lord, you delivered to me five talents; look, I have gained five more talents besides them.' His lord said to him, 'Well done, good and faithful servant; you were faithful over a few things, I will make you ruler over many things. Enter into the joy of your lord.' He also who had received two talents came and said, 'Lord, you delivered to me two talents; look, I have gained two more talents besides them.' His lord said to him, 'Well done, good and faithful servant; you have been faithful over a few things, I will make you ruler over many things. Enter into the joy of your lord.' "Then he who had received the one talent came and said, 'Lord, I knew you to be a hard man, reaping where you have not sown, and gathering where you have not scattered seed. And I was afraid, and went and hid your talent in the ground. Look, there you have what is yours.' "But his lord answered and said to him, 'You wicked and lazy servant, you knew that I reap where I have not sown, and gath-

er where I have not scattered seed. So you ought to have deposited my money with the bankers, and at my coming I would have received back my own with interest. So take the talent from him, and give it to him who has ten talents. 'For to everyone who has, more will be given, and he will have abundance; but from him who does not have, even what he has will be taken away. And cast the unprofitable servant into the outer darkness. There will be weeping and gnashing of teeth.'

It is interesting to note the reason that He gave this parable. He was approaching Jerusalem and many thought that He was going to become King of Israel and overthrow the Roman military occupation when He entered Jerusalem—verse 11

He then used this parable to bring clarity that His Kingdom was not going to appear immediately and as a result of that they should do BUSINESS with what He had given until His return.

In this parable Christ is represented by the nobleman and the Believers are represented by the servants or slaves.

It describes Christ's departure from the earth to receive His Kingdom and return on the specific day pre-ordained by The Father.

LET'S GO INTO THE PARABLE
Before leaving, the nobleman calls his servants and the distribution of resources is made.

There are FOUR CATEGORIES of servants, and each of them were given a different amount of minas.

The term mina is a Semitic word that means both a weight and a sum of money in Israel, Egypt and ancient Greece.

It was worth about 100 shekels or 100 drachmas or one-sixtieth of a talent.

It represented 100 days' wages. In weight it was about 15 ounces and was valued around $30.00 CND and that was over 2000 years ago. That was a significant amount of money back then.

So they were given quite a large sum of money. This could be typified as us being given many gifts and talents by the Holy Spirit. However, let us proceed in downloading principles from this account.

DO BUSINESS
The nobleman then told them to do business until his return.

The phrase **DO BUSINESS** IS A TRANSLATION OF THE Greek PRAGMATEUOMAI and it means *to accomplish by economic traffic or to gain by trading*. Let's go a bit deeper here: our English word pragmatic comes from the first part of the Greek—pragma, which means business.

PRAGMATIC—BEING PRACTICAL OR BUSINESSLIKE
So here we see the nobleman and a type of Christ telling his servants also a type of the Believer to use the talents that were given to gain increase for him. He is telling them that through economic trafficking and trading they should gain an increase for him.

Now this is very interesting and as such we should briefly note this. Remember, Lucifer was cast out of Heaven because he tapped into this dynamic of using what he was given to trade and make an increase. However, his problem was that he used what God had given him to traffic and trade and realized great returns, but he took it for himself and to be used in an attempt to take over God's place and for that he was cast out—Ezekiel 28:1-5, 11-18

> *The word of the LORD came to me again, saying, "Son of man, say to the prince of Tyre, 'Thus says the Lord GOD: "Because your heart is lifted up, And you say, 'I am a god, I sit in the seat of gods, In the midst of the seas,' Yet you are a man, and not a god, Though you set your heart as the heart of a god (Behold, you are wiser than Daniel! There is no secret that can be hidden from you! With your wisdom and your understanding You have gained riches for yourself, And gathered gold and silver into your treasuries; By your great wisdom in trade you have increased your riches, And your heart is lifted up because of your riches),"*
>
> *Moreover the word of the LORD came to me, saying, "Son of man, take up a lamentation for the king of Tyre, and say to him, 'Thus says the Lord GOD: "You were the seal of perfection, Full of wisdom and perfect in beauty. You were in Eden, the garden of God; Every precious stone was your covering: The sardius, topaz, and diamond, Beryl, onyx, and jasper, Sapphire, turquoise, and emerald with gold. The workmanship of your timbrels and pipes Was prepared for you*

on the day you were created. "You were the anointed cherub who covers; I established you; You were on the holy mountain of God; You walked back and forth in the midst of fiery stones. You were perfect in your ways from the day you were created, Till iniquity was found in you. "By the abundance of your trading You became filled with violence within, And you sinned; Therefore I cast you as a profane thing Out of the mountain of God; And I destroyed you, O covering cherub, From the midst of the fiery stones. "Your heart was lifted up because of your beauty; You corrupted your wisdom for the sake of your splendor; I cast you to the ground, I laid you before kings, That they might gaze at you. "You defiled your sanctuaries By the multitude of your iniquities, By the iniquity of your trading; Therefore I brought fire from your midst; It devoured you, And I turned you to ashes upon the earth In the sight of all who saw you.

For this reason it is vitally important for us to understand that we are to use what the Lord has blessed us with to gain increase for His Kingdom and His purpose in the earth!

THE NOBLEMAN'S RETURN—EVALUATION TIME

The nobleman returns and calls for his servants so that they might give an account of their stewardship.

THE FIRST GROUP

This servant has done spectacular—he has an increase factor of 10 or 1000% increase. Being faithful in money matters he is awarded ten cities.

THE SECOND GROUP

This servant has also done well and has an increase factor of 5 or 500% and as such is given authority over five cities. There is consistency with the reward system thus far.

THE THIRD GROUP

This servant is very interesting. He fails to trade and make an increase with what he was given and boldly declares why he did not. Her are the reasons:

1. He was afraid of the nobleman because of an inaccurate perception and negative view of him. This reveals to us that there was no relationship and as such incorrect assumptions were made.
2. He saw the nobleman as a hard or exacting man. He declared to him—You are too severe in your dealings. In essence, you are not nice and too mean!
3. He accuses the nobleman of taking up where he had not laid down and reaping where he had not sown. In essence what he was saying was that the nobleman was in the habit of unjustly appropriating the increase of other men's labour. (Obviously he had no clue as to what the nobleman intended to give in exchange for all the hard work)
4. He did not trust the nobleman and therefore sought to avoid perceived punishment resulting from any possible loss of investment—(this was due to the incorrect perception that all he wanted was increase so that he could take it for himself)

THE NOBLEMAN'S RESPONSE TO THIS SERVANT
First to begin with we see that this servant was about to get exactly what he expected—His master replied, I will judge you by your own words.

He was then rebuked for not entrusting his master's money to the bank in order that it would gain some interest. This is interesting as Christ viewed **the drawing of interest from the bank as a MINIMUM level of activity for a fearful person to accomplish**.

However, this is not what was expected from his faithful servants. He expected multiplication. This leads us to understand that:

FINANCIAL PASSIVITY WILL NOT BRING THE KIND OF INCREASE JESUS EXPECTS US TO. This principle holds true for every area of our lives. Passivity is not a Kingdom Quality. We can quote numerous Scriptures to back that up—From the days of John the Baptist until now the Kingdom of God is forcefully advanced and forceful men press into it—Matthew 11:11-12, Luke 16:16. They that know their God shall be strong and do great exploits—Daniel 11:32, etc., etc., etc....

Christ expects us to actively invest and have multiplication of the resources that He gives us—2 Peter 1:5-11, we are expected to ADD to our FAITH, that's where it all begins, we have all been given the same measure of initial FAITH, and any reluctance to add to what God has given is a sure sign of FEAR and not FAITH!!!

The master goes on to also call him wicked—however, in Matthew's account he is described as LAZY. Lazy comes from the Greek word **okneros** which is rendered—one who shirks his duty, inactive, idle, or a refusal to work—a condition condemned by many biblical writers. "Because of laziness the building decays," wrote the author of Ecclesiastes, "and through idleness of hands the house leaks" (Ecclesiastes 10:18).

So then the real reason behind this servant's lack of increase and productivity is his LAZINESS!!!

FOURTH GROUP
This group of the other seven servants refused to have the nobleman as king over them. This represents those Believers who refuse to have Jesus as King and Lord over every area of their lives including their FINANCES.

Obviously, they received the money, and it would suggest that they spent it on themselves because unlike the Third Group they did not return the money.

The outcome—the master commanded that they be killed right in his sight. Depart from me I never knew you, you workers of iniquity.

CONCLUSION—THE PRINCIPLE OF MOMENTUM
Both Luke and Matthew's account reported that the mina from the Third servant was taken away from him and given to the First who had the trading factor of 10. This prompted the bystanders to cry foul, unfair, and unjust: Luke 19:26

For I say to you that to everyone who has, more will be given. And from him who has not, even that which he has will be taken from him.

This is powerful and profound. You see, Christ will always reward fruitfulness and faithfulness with additional resources, either spiritual (more revelation, etc.) or naturally (finances, people, etc.) or both.

This is momentum! The more we use what the Lord has given us the more we will receive causing greater growth and abundance to take place! HALLELUJAH!!!

Remember when we came to the end of the Parable of The Rich Young Ruler Jesus made a statement that seemed to be totally unrelated to the context; and only Matthew picks it up – In Matthew 19:30 Jesus declares "However, many who are first will be last, and many who are last will be first."

This had to do with what He was about to teach them and once again it had to do with money. Remarkably interesting to note is that a majority of Jesus' parables were about money or wealth of some sort.

Matthew then goes on to report the next parable Jesus spoke to them about. Let us explore the parable of the vineyard.

LET'S CHECK OUR UNDERSTANDING OF CHAPTER 7—THE PARABLE OF THE TEN MINAS

1. What does the Scripture say is the reason for the parable that Jesus spoke to His disciples in Matthew 25:14-30 and Luke 19:11-26?
2. According to this parable what is expected of His disciples/today's Believers while they wait for the King of the Kingdom to establish His rule on earth?
3. What is the Greek word "Pragmateuomai" translated into in this parable? What does this Greek word literally mean?
4. Who are the four groups of servants/Believers that Jesus is talking about in this parable?
5. What type of reward system was used by the Master in rewarding His servants/Believers?
6. What strikes you about the third group of Believers/servants who failed to trade and make an increase? What reasons did they put forth for not having traded and done as instructed by their master?
7. How did the Master respond to this servant who failed to carry out his instructions to trade and make increase for him, with the Minas he was given?
8. How did Christ view drawing interest from the Bank?
9. According to this parable does Christ expect us, His Believers to just draw an interest on the resources He has placed within our care or should we go out boldly and take calculated risks knowing that we are backed by the owner and author of all resources?
10. According to 2 Peter 1:5-11, we are to Add to our Faith. What could be the single most powerful reason for us to either fail or excel in this area?

11. Who consists of the fourth group of Believers described in this parable? What was their reward?
12. Which of the operating principles of God's Kingdom, is Jesus trying to teach us though this parable?
13. Fill in the Blanks:
    Christ will always reward f _ _ _ _ _ _ _ _ _ _ s and f _ _ _ _ _ _ _ _ _ _ s with additional resources, either s _ _ _ _ _ _ _ l or n _ _ _ _ _ l or both. This is momentum! The more we u _ _ what the Lord has g _ _ _ n us the more we will r _ _ _ _ _ e causing greater g _ _ _ _ h and a _ _ _ _ _ _ _ e to take place.

CHAPTER EIGHT
THE PARABLE OF THE VINEYARD

MATTHEW 20:1-16 NIV

> "For the kingdom of heaven is like a landowner who went out early in the morning to hire workers for his vineyard. He agreed to pay them a denarius for the day and sent them into his vineyard. "About nine in the morning he went out and saw others standing in the marketplace doing nothing. He told them, 'You also go and work in my vineyard, and I will pay you whatever is right.' So, they went. "He went out again about noon and about three in the afternoon and did the same thing. About five in the afternoon, he went out and found still others standing around. He asked them, 'Why have you been standing here all day long doing nothing?' "'Because no one has hired us,' they answered. "He said to them, 'You also go and work in my vineyard.' "When evening came, the owner of the vineyard said to his foreman, 'Call the workers and pay them their wages, beginning with the last ones hired and going on to the first.' "The workers who were hired about five in the afternoon came and each received a denarius. So when those came who were hired first, they expected to receive more. But each one of them also received a denarius. When they received it, they began to grumble against the landowner. 'These who were hired last worked only one hour,' they said, 'and you have made them equal to us who have borne the

burden of the work and the heat of the day.' "But he answered one of them, 'I am not being unfair to you, friend. Didn't you agree to work for a denarius? Take your pay and go. I want to give the one who was hired last the same as I gave you. Don't I have the right to do what I want with my own money? Or are you envious because I am generous?' "So, the last will be first, and the first will be last."

As in so many of His parables, Christ is describing the rule of the Kingdom of Heaven upon the earth by means of comparison.

In this parable, Christ presents Himself as the landowner with a vineyard and Believers as the workers that are hired.

There are five groups of workers represented and we will look at them:

The first group he hires agrees for a specified wage—this is very important!

The second, third and fourth groups of workers were found idling and were hired—verses 3-5—the third, sixth and ninth hour. However, something different occurred with these three groups, all the landowner promised them was to pay them what was right and to this they agreed and went to work. This establishes the fact that they TRUSTED the landowner to be fair.

Group Five:

At the eleventh hour he goes out and finds yet another group standing idly by, and he enters a conversation with them, asking them the reason for their idleness; to which they replied—no one had hired them. They were idle for almost the entire working day. They were without purpose and the landowner gave them purpose and told them to go and work.

The interesting thing about this group as recorded in the NIV—Matthew 20:17; is that they are told to go to work without any promise of a wage and they went. They were just happy to be given work, purpose, and a vision. They were idle, no one hired them and now they have been given purposeful work; they were not primarily interested in the money.

I sense that they said to themselves—this is the eleventh hour; no one has hired us before now, the fact that this landowner is willing to hire us at this late hour we are grateful and will trust him because he did not have to do it. Money obviously is not an issue with him so we will not make it an issue either, because we could have gone all day without any work and without any wages. They completely trusted the landowner—Powerful stuff!

THE TWELFTH HOUR—SALARY AND WAGES TIME
The first thing that we notice is the order is reversed—the last group of workers is called first for their wages. This is interesting on several fronts:

1. They were not promised any wages but trusted the landowner and were willing to work for nothing.
2. They completely trusted the landowner and they are being rewarded for it.
3. The landowner was going to use them to teach an invaluable lesson to all concerned.

In our next four chapters we would be looking at principles of wealth and prosperity.

LET'S CHECK OUR UNDERSTANDING OF CHAPTER 8—THE PARABLE OF THE VINEYARD
1. What is Christ describing through the parable of "The Vinyard" recorded in Matthew 20:1-16?
2. Who are the five different types of workers that were hired?
3. How will you describe the difference between the employment contract the owner (Christ) entered, with each of these groups?
4. Why would the last group of workers to have been employed, were eager to accept the offer of work even without an upfront payment agreement?
5. What happens at the twelfth hour? What are the key factors of interest?

CHAPTER NINE
PRINCIPLES OF WEALTH AND PROSPERITY - ONE

We would be doing an in-depth study of Wealth and Prosperity as I truly sense the Father wants us to fully understand this before He pours out His increase upon us.

Let us begin by saying that God is the source of our resources... Yes, He IS. Another thing we need to know is this: God is not limited to our understanding, but He is always inviting us into HIS understanding! And we need to not only know this, but we need to totally believe this. Because without Him we are nothing... Here is what 1 Chronicles 29:12 says: I like how deceased Dr. Tim Early interprets this:

> Both riches (wealth,—from another Hebrew word which means "to accumulate, to grow, make rich) and honor (weight, splendor, glory) come of (or from) thee, and thou reignest (to rule, have dominion, governor, have power) over all; and in thine hand is power (to be firm, vigor, capacity, means, produce, force, might, strength, wealth) and might (force, valor, victory, mastery, strength—from another Hebrew word which means "powerful, warrior, champion, chief, excel, tyrant, giant, strong man, valiant man"); and in thine hand it is to make great (advance, bring up, exceed, increase, magnify, nourish up, promote), and to give strength (to fasten upon, cure, help, repair, fortify...) unto all. End of quote

The time is now to declare apostolically and prophetically and to demonstrate present day truth that God the Father is pouring into the corporate Body of Christ supernatural wealth and prosperity to advance the Kingdom of God, to also meet the needs of the Saints, and for us to purposefully enjoy, all unto the praises of His glory!

With all this in mind, you can choose to do one of two things:

1. dismiss this truth and say that all wealth leads to covetousness or
2. accept the truth and say it can power-fuel the very purpose of God for administrating His resources in the earth.

For the two main tangible and powerful requirements in advancing the Kingdom are:

1. Kingdom people and
2. Kingdom finances/resources.

And to support just how important the proper allocation and stewardship of money is, it would be good for us to turn and read Ecclesiastes 10:19.

The officials make a feast for enjoyment [instead of repairing what is broken], and serve wine to make life merry, and money is the answer to everything. AMP

In this teaching I would like to impart prophetically into our hearing the word of the Lord concerning Wealth and Prosperity.

We declare that God is pouring into and is ready to increase the flow of wealth and resources into many Saints. Resources and tangible prosperity not only in heralding the Gospel of the Lord Jesus Christ, but into the very life of His people to enjoy the good of the land.

And I do believe that we all know and understand this but let me say it again: True prosperity is not only in the temporal and physical dimension, but also, spiritual, and there are contingent blessings of prosperity for His people.

However, let's focus on the truth which is, that God is not against us having to enjoy the provisions of His wealth and prosperity in His season and in HIS way, but simply admonishes us to guard our heart against covetousness (greed), and our dependency and trust in tangible riches and resources.

LET GOD BE TRUE...
For Centuries, the popular belief held among many Believers was...

> "If you really love the Lord and want to serve Him in all humility, you have to live in a vow of poverty!" If you love the Lord, you can't afford to be rich (or be enriched) as this will bring a snare to your soul!" If you want to make it to Heaven, you must give up all of your goods to prove worthy and fit for eternity!" If you are rich, materially prosperous and wealthy, give it all away as this will become a stumbling-block to many, even your own self!" And, if you are ever found praying and thanking God for the super-abundant provisions of the Lord for His people in any form, shape, or fashion, then forget it, because Jesus is coming soon, and we won't have the time to be enjoying it anyway! In fact, we should be thinking of souls and not the sales in the store! Just Jesus, and nothing else really matters!"

Oh, I tell you that the spirit of poverty is accentuated, or heightened through such commonly held beliefs as these, with a hidden agenda to diminish the capacities of the Saints in advancing the Kingdom. For as long as the Church remains in fear of sin through the accumulation of purposeful material wealth, then the supernatural dimension of wealth and prosperity will be potentially hindered in many, from its rightful use and appropriation in the corporate Body of Christ and in the destiny of nations.

Nevertheless, God has a word for our wealth and prosperity, and it is time that we heard the conclusion of the whole matter before dismissing the whole thing altogether.

We need to be open to the voice of the Lord in His appointed leaders and not become skeptic for the few that have veered off the right path. For this message and ministry of God's supernatural provision is one accompanied with signs, wonders, miracles, and mighty deeds. It shall astound and convince many that God is our source, in both the tangible and intangible blessings.

GUARDING AGAINST COVETOUSNESS AND TRUST IN WEALTH AND RICHES

We would be looking at some Scriptural references to encourage our hearts to have the motive and mind of the Kingdom, which is love.

In 1 Corinthians 13, we understand that love is a person, and God so loved that He gave, according to John 3:16. Love, the motive and heartbeat of the Kingdom, endures long, is kind, envies not, not arrogant, or boisterous, nor is it a braggart. Love personified (Christ Jesus) and the motive of the Kingdom does not behave itself in an indecent manner, does not seek its own, not easily provoked, thinks, or ponders no evil, nor does it rejoice in sin or iniquity. Love rejoices in the truth, bear all things, believe all things, hope all things, and endure all things. It is a life manifesting consistently God's unending and abounding love.

Unlike lust, which is compulsory, love gives!

In this section, I would like for us to first look at the negative uses of wealth, riches, and prosperity.

In our next section, we will further establish the laws and principles of prosperity, even God's will to enjoy abundant life here on earth. John 10:10; 3 John 2-4; Deuteronomy 8:18 from the Amplified Version.

John 10:10 AMP

The thief comes only in order to steal and kill and destroy. I came that they may have and enjoy life, and have it in abundance [to the full, till it overflows].

3 John 2-4 AMP

Beloved, I pray that in every way you may succeed and prosper and be in good health [physically], just as [I know] your soul prospers [spiritually]. For I was greatly pleased when [some of the] brothers came [from time to time] and testified to your [faithfulness to the] truth [of the gospel message], that is, how you are walking in truth. I have no greater joy than this, to hear that my [spiritual] children are living [their lives] in the truth.

Deuteronomy 8:18 AMP

But you shall remember [with profound respect] the LORD your God, for it is He who is giving you power to make wealth, that He may confirm His covenant which He swore [solemnly promised] to your fathers, as it is this day.

NEGATIVE USES OF WEALTH
Job 21:13-15 and all the following passages are taken from the KJV, unless otherwise stated.

They spend their days in wealth, and in a moment go down to the grave. Therefore, they say unto God, Depart from us; we desire not the knowledge of your ways. What is the Almighty, that we should serve him? And what profit should we have if we pray unto him?

Proverbs 18:11

The rich man's wealth is his strong city, and as a high wall in his own conceit.

Proverbs 28:11

The rich man is wise in his own conceit...

Jeremiah 9:23

Thus says the Lord...let not the rich man glory in his riches.

Ezekiel 7:19

They shall cast their silver in the streets, and their gold shall be removed. Their silver and their gold shall not be able to deliver them in the day of the wrath of the Lord; they shall not satisfy their souls, neither fill their bowels: because it is the stumbling block of their iniquity.

Ezekiel 28:5

By thy great wisdom and by thy traffic have thou increased thy riches, and your heart is lifted up because of thy riches.

Matthew 19:24 **[this is one that so many use to embrace their poverty mentality]**

It is easier for a camel to go through the eye of a needle, than for a rich man to enter into the kingdom of God.

Mark 10:21-23 **[and also this one]**

Then Jesus beholding him loved him, and said unto him, One thing you lack: go your way, sell whatever you have, and give to the poor, and you shall have treasure in heaven: and come, take up the cross, and follow me. And he was sad at that saying, and went away grieved: for he had great possessions. And Jesus looked round about, and said unto his disciples, How hardly shall they that have riches enter into the kingdom of God.

Luke 6:24-25

Woe unto you that are rich! For you have received your consolation. Woe unto you that are full! For you shall hunger.

Luke 12:15-21

And he (Jesus) said unto them, Take heed, and beware of <u>covetousness</u>: for a man's life consists not in the abundance of things, which he possesses. And he thought within himself, saying, What shall I do, because I have no room where to bestow my fruits And he said, This will I do: I will pull down my barns, and build greater; and there will I bestow all my fruits and my goods. And I will say to my soul, Soul, thou hast much goods laid up for many years; take thine ease, eat, drink, and be merry. But God said unto him, Thou fool, this night thy soul shall be required of thee: then whose *shall those things be, which thou hast provided? So is he that layeth up treasure for himself, and is not rich toward God.* [Emphasis Author's]

Luke 16:13-14

No man can serve two masters: for either he will hate the one, and love the other, or else he will hold to the one, and despise the other. You cannot serve God and Mammon [money]. And the Pharisees also, who were covetous heard all these things... [Parenthesis Author's]

1 Timothy 6:17

Charge them that are rich in this world, that they be not high-minded, nor trust in uncertain riches, but the living God, who gives richly all things to enjoy.

Proverbs 23:4-5

Labor not to be rich: cease from your own wisdom. Will you set your eyes upon that which is nothing? For riches certainly make themselves wings; they fly away as an eagle toward heaven.

Jeremiah 48:36

Therefore, my heart shall sound for Moab like pipes, and my heart shall sound like pipes for the men of Kirheres: because the riches that he has gotten are perished.

Mark 4:19

And the cares of this world, and the deceitfulness of riches, and the lusts of other things entering in, choke out the word, and it becomes unfruitful.

1 Timothy 6:4, 5, 6, 7, 9, 10

For he is proud...supposing that gain is godliness: from such withdraw yourself. <u>But godliness with contentment is great gain</u>. For we brought nothing into this world, and it is certain we can carry nothing out...But they that be rich fall into temptation and a snare, and into many foolish and hurtful lusts, which drown men in destruction and perdition. For the love of money is the root of all evil: which while some coveted after, they have erred from the faith, and pierced themselves through with many sorrows. [Emphasis Author's]

Let us end this chapter by reading these passages: James 2:5-7; 5:1-5; and 1 John 3:17

Listen, my beloved brethren: Has God not chosen the poor of this world to be rich in faith and heirs of the kingdom which He promised to those who love Him? But you have dishonored the poor man. Do not the rich oppress you and drag you into the courts? Do they not blaspheme that noble name by which you are called?

Come now, you rich, weep and howl for your miseries that are coming upon you! Your riches are corrupted, and your garments are moth-eaten. Your gold and silver are corroded, and their corrosion will be a witness against you and will eat your flesh like fire. You have heaped up treasure in the last days. Indeed, the wages of the laborers who mowed your fields, which you kept back by fraud, cry out; and the cries of the reapers have reached the ears of the Lord of Sabaoth. You have lived on the earth in pleasure and luxury; you have fattened your hearts as in a day of slaughter.

But whoever has this world's goods, and sees his brother in need, and shuts up his heart from him, how does the love of God abide in him?

LET'S CHECK OUR UNDERSTANDING OF CHAPTER 9—PRINCIPLES OF WEALTH AND PROSPERITY—ONE

1. Do you agree that God is the source of our resources? Explain.
2. When it comes to inheriting wealth from the giver of all things, God the Father, what options do we have before us?
3. What are the two main requirements in advancing the Kingdom of God in the earth?
4. The author says: "Tru prosperity is not only in the temporal and physical dimension, but also spiritual, and there are contingent blessings of prosperity for His people". Do you agree with this saying? Why?
5. Are you of the opinion that God is against us having and enjoying wealth and prosperity?
6. What is it that God wants us to be careful of in this area of tangible riches and resources?
7. What could happen if we become skeptic about the message and ministry of God's supernatural provision?
8. What are some of the ways that we should not be using the resources and riches that God blesses us with? Explain with Scriptural references.
9. According to James 2:5-7; 5:1-5; and 1 John 3:17 what is expected of us as rich Believers and Kingdom Citizens?

CHAPTER TEN
PRINCIPLES OF WEALTH AND PROSPERITY - TWO

OK, SO LET US NOW LOOK AT THE: LAWS AND PRINCIPLES OF PROSPERITY

The laws and principles of prosperity are built into creation itself. Many ungodly men and women have tapped into Kingdom principles and have amassed millions of dollars for their personal success.

Relationship experts, motivational speakers, peak performance lecturers, entrepreneurs, and many others have practiced some of the principles, which characterize or reveal in part or parcel these divine laws. From coaches of major league sports teams to home managers from the most remote places of the earth, these laws and principles have been practiced for Centuries and are not to be anything entirely new to Us the Saints. And Kingdom principles are not exclusive to someone being a Christian either.

According to Genesis 8:22, (While the earth remains, Seedtime and harvest, Cold and heat Winter and summer, And day and night Shall not cease.) There is the first mention of the law of **Seed, Time,** and **Harvest.**

I know that this passage states **seedtime,** but I would like to break that word up in this teaching: **Seed, Time,** and **Harvest** as I do believe that when we sow our seeds there must be a time lapse before we can receive a harvest.

This major Kingdom principle is found in the development of every living thing in earth, sky, and sea. The law of seed, time, and harvest is a perpetual one, and is noted among farmers, who, in the understanding of many present truth ministers, have one of the closest earthly professions (and functionalities) to God. Let us look at several passages that confirm this:

Mark 4:26-29

And He said, "The kingdom of God is as if a man should scatter seed on the ground, and should sleep by night and rise by day, and the seed should sprout and grow, he himself does not know how. For the earth yields crops by itself: first the blade, then the head, after that the full grain in the head. But when the grain ripens, immediately he puts in the sickle, because the harvest has come."

Matthew 13:19-23, 24-30, 31-32

When anyone hears the word of the kingdom, and does not understand it, then the wicked one comes and snatches away what was sown in his heart. This is he who received seed by the wayside. But he who received the seed on stony places, this is he who hears the word and immediately receives it with joy; yet he has no root in himself but endures only for a while. For when tribulation or persecution arises because of the word, immediately he stumbles. Now he who received seed among the thorns is he who hears the word, and the cares of this world and the deceitfulness of riches choke the word, and he becomes unfruitful. But he who received seed on the good ground is he who hears the word and understands it, who indeed bears fruit and produces: some a hundredfold, some sixty, some thirty."

Another parable He put forth to them, saying: "The kingdom of heaven is like a man who sowed good seed in his field; but while men slept, his enemy came and sowed tares among the wheat and went his way. But when the grain had sprouted and produced a crop, then the tares also appeared. So, the servants of the owner came and said to him, 'Sir, did you not sow good seed in your field? How then does it have tares?' He said to them, 'An enemy has done this.' The servants said to him, 'Do you want us then to go and gather them up?' But he said, 'No, lest while you gather up the tares you also uproot the wheat with them. Let both grow together until the harvest, and at the time of harvest I will say to the reapers, "First gather together the tares and bind them in bundles to burn them, but gather the wheat into my barn." ' "

Another parable He put forth to them, saying: "The kingdom of heaven is like a mustard seed, which a man took and sowed in his field, which indeed is the least of all the seeds; but when it is grown it is greater than the herbs and becomes a tree, so that the birds of the air come and nest in its branches."

John 12:24

Most assuredly, I say to you, unless a grain of wheat falls into the ground and dies, it remains alone; but if it dies, it produces much grain.

And our very lives can be inventoried/or listed by a process of development through seed, time, and harvest. If we sow attitudes of fear and frustration, we reap it. If we sow hate, bitterness, and discord, we reap it. If we sow doubt, confusion, and worry, we reap it. If we sow gossip and backbiting, we will surely reap it! That's seed, time, and harvest, good or bad, positive, or seemingly negative. (as recorded in Galatians 6:7-8)

Do not be deceived, God is not mocked; for whatever a man sows, that he will also reap. For he who sows to his flesh will of the flesh reap corruption, but he who sows to the Spirit will of the Spirit reap everlasting life.

On the other hand, if we sow the fruit of the Spirit, we will reap it. If we sow intercession of others, we will reap intercession. If we sow faith, we will reap it. If we sow hospitality, generosity, and kindness we reap it. If we sow mercy, we will reap it.

Whatever we sow, we simply reap! (See Acts 4:34-37; 5:1-11) we all know this account but for purpose of teaching, let us read them again:

Nor was there anyone among them who lacked; for all who were possessors of lands or houses sold them and brought the proceeds of the things that were sold, and laid them at the apostles' feet; and they distributed to each as anyone had need. And Joses, who was also named Barnabas by the apostles (which is translated Son of Encouragement), a Levite of the country of Cyprus, having land, sold it, and brought the money and laid it at the apostles' feet.

But a certain man named Ananias, with Sapphira his wife, sold a possession. And he kept back part of the proceeds, his wife also being aware of it, and brought a certain part and laid it at the apostles' feet. But Peter said, "Ananias, why has Satan filled your heart to lie to the Holy Spirit and keep back part of the price of the land for yourself? While it remained, was it not your own? And after it was sold, was it not in your own control? Why have you conceived this thing in your heart? You have not lied to men but to God." Then Ananias, hearing these words, fell down and breathed his last. So great fear came upon all those who heard these things. And the young men arose and wrapped him up, carried him out, and buried him. Now it was about three hours later when his wife came in, not knowing what had happened. And Peter answered her, "Tell me whether you sold the land for so much?" She said, "Yes, for so much." Then Peter said to her, "How is it that you have agreed together to test the Spirit of the Lord? Look, the feet of those who have buried your husband are at the door, and they will carry you out." Then immediately she fell down at his feet and breathed her last. And the young men came in and found her dead, and carrying her out, buried her by her husband. So great fear came upon all the church and upon all who heard these things.

Next, we will be looking into Five Important Laws with Governing Principles—Each for HIS Prosperity for our LIVES—we would be looking into these in a bit, but first:
- It is the will of God to prosper His people.
- It is His will to see us joyful, happy, blessed, healthy, and having all our needs met according to HIS RICHES and HIS GLORY! (See Philippians 4:11-13, 17-19).

- We are not measuring ourselves by ourselves in accordance with what we think one another should be by the conventional and worldly wisdom. Not so, we are simply stating that God's plan of prosperity and wealth has specific purposes, and specific seasons of increase and abundance.

We also need to understand that prophetically, one must know their season, discern the times, and to move ahead according to what the Lord has tailor-made in expression for one's life. **All are not going to be multi-millionaires, but it should not stop us from operating *in* Kingdom principles and spiritual laws anyway**.

3 John 2-4

Beloved, I wish above all things thou you may prosper and be in health, even as your soul prospers (the whole man). For I rejoiced greatly, when the brethren came and testified of the truth that is in you, even as you walk in the truth. I have no greater joy than to hear that my children walk in the truth.

The words prosper here means *"to help on the road, pass, succeed in reaching, figuratively, to succeed in business affairs, and to have a prosperous journey."*

It is not a bad word at all. It only appears sinful when men abuse the principles of the word or turn away from God altogether. And, when there is trust in one's own riches and wealth, or the accumulation of riches through covetousness or greed, in this you will find a more negative connotation of the word "prosperity."

Nevertheless, prosperity is not inherently evil, nor is having money. It is what you do with what you have, as God is the True Owner, and we are the stewards. Stewardship is the key principle here in how prosperity is received and dispensed. If we misapply God's laws in HIS prosperity, we could easily abuse or misuse the resources and provisions given and become ineffective in advancing the Kingdom.

Now, let's define the word prosper, prosperous, and prosperity from the overview of Scripture, as we reference in part some of these scriptural definitions...

Genesis 24:40

The Lord, before whom I walk, will send his angel with you, and prosper (to push forward, break out, go over, be profitable) *your way (or in essence: make things work out).* [Emphasis Author's]

Joshua 1:7

...that you may prosper (to be circumspect, to be intelligent, consider, expert, instruct, give skill, have good success, make understand) *wherever you go.* [Emphasis Author's]

2 Chronicles 26:5

...God made him to prosper. (to push forward) [Emphasis Author's]

Nehemiah 2:20

...The God of heaven, he will prosper us. (push forward) [Emphasis Author's]

Isaiah 55:11

...it shall prosper (push forward) *in the thing whereto he sends it.* [Emphasis Author's]

Psalms 122:6

...they shall prosper (to be tranquil, secure or successful, be happy, be in safety) *that love you...* [Emphasis Author's]

Judges 4:24

...and the hand of the children of Israel prospered.

Job 36:11

If they obey and serve him, they shall spend their days in prosperity (good, a good thing, well, better, cheerful, bountiful), *and their years in pleasures.* [Emphasis Author's]

Psalms 35:27

...Let the Lord be magnified, which has pleasure in the prosperity (Hebrew – safe, well, happy, health, welfare, peace) *of his servants.* [Emphasis Author's]

Psalms 118:25

...Lord, I beseech you, send now prosperity (break out, push forward, go over, akin to another word to advance) [Emphasis Author's]

Psalms 122:7

Peace be within your walls, and prosperity (security, abundance, quietness) within your palaces. [Emphasis Author's]

Isaiah 48:15

I, even I, have spoken; yea, I have called him: I have brought him, and he shall make his way prosperous (break out, go over). [Emphasis Author's]

2 Chronicles 7:11

...and in his own house, he prosperously effected (break out, go over, push forward). [Emphasis Author's]

In essence we see that GOD's nature is prosperity and this is not limited to only money. Money is a means, but God is the source and resource, therefore, Prosperity is first spirit, then soul, then body. God promises in

His word to make our way prosperous and to have good success or to do wisely, as we apply and appropriate the provisions of HIS word.

1 Samuel 2:7-8

The Lord makes poor, and makes rich: he brings low, and lifts up. He raises up the poor out of the dust, and lifts up the beggar from the dunghill, to set them among princes, and to make them inherit the throne of glory:

Here, the Lord promotes as in Psalms 75:6-7

For promotion cometh neither from the east, nor from the west, nor from the south. But God is the judge: he putteth down one, and setteth up another. KJV

After all this is Who God is: He puts one down and sets up another. He is gracious to those who are gracious, and merciful to the ones who are merciful. He is God and changes not in character. He's not governed by time and cannot be confined or conformed to external affairs. He is God all by Himself...

Now, let us explore the **Five Important Laws with Governing Principles Each for HIS Prosperity for our LIFE**

1—PROSPERITY IS THE WILL OF GOD, FOR US IN SPIRIT, SOUL, AND BODY.

I believe that is to teach that God wants us (the Born-Again Believer) whole in our spirit and soul, and not only in our body. The more Saints get a hold of this, the further we can:

1. advance the Gospel of the Kingdom abroad and
2. meet specific needs as apostolic ambassadors and humanitarians on the earth.

This, I truly believe is an important two-fold use of the prosperity of His servants.

2—PRAYER THROUGH FAITH WITH APPOINTED ACTION BASED ON GOD'S WORD AND WILL FOR YOUR LIFE HELPS TO OPERATE THE LAWS OR PRINCIPLES OF HIS PROSPERITY

Hebrews 11:6 says,

For without faith it is impossible to please him, for he which comes to God must believe, and that he is a "rewarder" of them which diligently seek him.

Faith is simply, a firm persuasion, and conviction based upon hearing. It is the assurance and confidence in God, the title deed, and the proof of what you don't see. Faith perceives as real what is not revealed to the senses. It is constantly before the Lord, in the Presence of Jesus Christ who is the Author and Finisher of our faith. See Hebrews 11:1, 3, 6; 12:2-3

According to Romans 1:16, it says: the *just shall live by faith...*
In Mark 11:24, Jesus says,

Therefore I say to you, whatever things you ask when you pray, believe that you receive them; and you will have them.

If God says it in His word, and you believe that it is for you based on the tailor-made will of God for your life, then Amen (So be it). You have the promise of the word, which is God Himself! (Yeah, and Amen)

3—PUTTING GOD FIRST AND FOREMOST IN YOUR LIFE

Matthew 6:33

But seek you first (and foremost) the kingdom of God, and his righteousness, and all of these things will be added unto you.

4—THE DIVINE LAW OF HONOURING THE LORD WITH OUR SUBSTANCE

Proverbs 3:9-10

Honour the Lord with your substance, and with the first fruits of all your increase: So shall your barns be filled with plenty, and your presses shall burst out with new wine.

5—THE SAINTS MUST RECOGNIZE THE PRINCIPLE OF SEED FOR SOWING AND BREAD FOR EATING:

Off the top ten means of becoming wealthy and prosperous in life is the principle of sowing seed... Besides investments, real estate, internet businesses, etc., sowing generously is a key method with purposeful cheerful giving. It is not always a matter of being led to give, but in having a heart to give. Life and gratitude is an attitude, and our attitude can determine our altitude (the height we climb to in God's Kingdom).

Beloved, giving is living, and living is giving!

Ecclesiastes 11:6

In the morning sow your seed, and in the evening, withhold not your hand...

In Genesis 26 Isaac sowed in famine and reaped 100-fold that same year!

In Luke 6:38 Jesus said,

Give, and it shall be given to you; good measure, pressed down, shaken together, and running over, shall men give into your bossom.

I am so reminded of the Saints of our house D-LIM, who continue to give of their time and talent unto the service of the Lord.

Now, the way you give is of your time, talents, and treasures. Even giving yourself to God as a reasonable sacrifice reveals in part your willingness to give of your substance. Why? For Giving is Living and Living is Giving!

Galatians 6:7-8 speaks of the law of sowing and reaping. 2 Corinthians 9:6 says,

If we give sparingly, we will reap sparingly, and if we sow bountifully, we will reap bountifully.

If Saints refuse to become givers IN God, then this shows a lack of generosity towards God, and suggest to the world that we serve a God who is least generous Himself, as we are the only true examples of God they have.
In truth, God is not moved merely by your needs alone but also by your seed!

LET'S CHECK OUR UNDERSTANDING OF CHAPTER 10—PRINCIPLES OF WEALTH AND PROSPERITY—TWO

1. Do you believe the laws and principles of prosperity are built into creation itself? Expound
2. Why are farmers considered to have the closest earthly profession to God?
3. What does the word prosper in 3 John 2-4 mean?
4. When does this prosperity turn evil?
5. How will the abuse or misuse of this prosperity affect the advancing of God's Kingdom upon the earth?
6. How do we know for a fact that God is the source of prosperity? Which Scriptures illude to this fact?
7. How then can we become prosperous?
8. Fill in the Blanks:
   This is who God is: He puts one d_ _ n and s_ _s up another. He is g_ _ _ _ _ _s to those who are g _ _ _ _ _ _ s, and merciful to the ones who are m _ _ _ _ _ _ l. He is God and changes not in c _ _ _ _ _ _ _ r. He's not g _ _ _ _ _ _ d by t _ _ e and cannot be c _ _ _ _ _ _ d or c _ _ _ _ _ _ _ d to external affairs. He is God all by Himself.
9. What are the five important laws and the governing principles of His Prosperity for our lives?
10. Why is it so important that we practice giving as recommended in 2 Corinthians 9:6?
11. What moves God to prosper us and to enjoy a wealthy life upon this earth?

CHAPTER ELEVEN
PRINCIPLES OF WEALTH AND PROSPERITY - THREE

GOD IS TRULY AMAZING, AND I JUST LOVE HIM WITH ALL OF MY HEART AND **my being. He is super wise.**

GOD'S KINGDOM ECONOMY AND WEALTH FACTOR.

Genesis 43:22

And other money have we brought down in our hands to buy food: we cannot tell who put our money in our sacks. (Today that could read—bank account, credit account, etc.) [Emphasis Author's]

God wants us supernaturally blessed and increased in all good things. In James 1:17 we see the following:

Every good gift and every perfect gift is from above, and comes down from the Father of lights, with whom there is no variation or shadow of turning.

We also see this truth in the following Passages:

Deuteronomy 12:7

You shall eat before the Lord your God, and you shall rejoice in all that you put your hand unto, you, and your households, wherein the Lord your God has blessed you.

1 Chronicles 1:12

Wisdom and knowledge is granted unto you; and I will give you riches, and wealth, and honor, such as none of the kings have had...

Job 22:18

He filled their houses with good things.

John 14:2

In My Father's house are many mansions; if it were not so, I would have told you. I go to prepare a place for you.

I believe that the Lord wants to fill our houses up with good things, furniture, beds, fabric, mirrors, food, clothing, shoes, and much more. This is a Covenant provision, and I also believe that this applies to our Spiritual houses, as well.

Psalms 34:10

They that <u>seek the Lord</u> shall not lack any good thing. [Emphasis Author's]

Psalms 68:19

Blessed be the Lord, who daily loads us with benefits...

Acts 14:17

He left not himself without witness, in that he did well and gave us rain from heaven, and fruitful seasons, filling our hearts with food and gladness.

POWER TO GET WEALTH

Deuteronomy 8:1-10

All the commandments which I command you this day shall you observe (be careful) to do, that you may live, and multiply, and go in and possess the land which the Lord promised to your fathers. And you shall remember all the way which the Lord your God led you these forty years in the wilderness, to humble you, and to test you, to learn what was in your heart, whether you would keep his commandments or not. <u>And he humbled you and suffered you to hunger, and fed you with manna, which you knew not; that he might make you know that man does not live by bread only, but by every word that proceeds out of the mouth of God does man live. Your raiment waxed not old upon you, nor did your foot swell, these forty years. You shall also consider (remember) in your heart</u>, *that, as a man chasten his son, so the Lord your God chastens you. Therefore, you shall keep the commandments of the Lord your God, to walk in his ways, and to fear him. For the Lord your God brings you into a good land, a land of brooks of water, of fountains and depths that spring out of valleys and hills: A land of wheat, and barley, and vines, and fig trees, and pomegranates; a land of oil olive, and honey. A land wherein you shall eat bread without scarceness, you shall not lack any thing in it; a land whose stones are iron, and out of whose hills you may dig brass. When you have eaten and are full, then you shall bless the Lord your God for the good land, which he has given you.* [Emphasis Author's]

Deuteronomy 8:17-18

And you say in your heart, my power and the might of my hand has gotten me this wealth. But you shall remember the Lord your God, for it is He that gives you power to get wealth, that He may establish (bring to pass) *His covenant which He swore unto your fathers* (I believe that this is generational), *as it is this day.* [Emphasis Author's]

Now, the principal understanding of Deuteronomy 8 reveals that supernatural wealth and prosperity comes from God, and not merely by our own means and external efforts such as working overtime or working two and three different jobs. This wealth is from the divine enablement and supernatural ability of the Spirit of God and is purposed to bring testimony and praise to the Lord throughout the earth.

Oh, let us seriously believe this Word of the Lord. He really is going to bless us as a house, abundantly—Just keep on seeking Him.

2 Chronicles 1:12

Wisdom and knowledge is granted unto you; and I will give you riches, and wealth...

The word *"wealth"* in Deuteronomy 8, and in a number of other Scriptures, is from the Hebrew word "Chayil (khay-yil) and is defined as *"force—whether of men, resources, or army—wealth, virtue, valor, strength, able, activity, band of men or soldiers, great company, goods, host, power, might, riches, virtuous."*

Even the **virtuous woman** [or Chayil woman] of Proverbs 31:10 holds the exact same Hebrew definition...

Who can find a virtuous wife? For her worth is far above rubies. [Emphasis Author's]

In the language of the Spirit, God is converting over to His people some serious resources, as is found in the following word Exodus 36:6-7.

So Moses gave a commandment, and they caused it to be proclaimed throughout the camp, saying, "Let neither man nor woman do any more work for the offering of the sanctuary." And the people were restrained from bringing, for the material they had was sufficient for all the work to be done—indeed too much.

Now that's a really interesting pattern of giving! To be restrained from Giving versus constraining others to give. O Lord, Help us! Let us pray that we can experience this level in our giving.

Proverbs 13:22 says.

A good man leaves an inheritance for his children's children: and the wealth of the sinner is laid up for the just.

I do believe that there is a conversion process going on in the Spirit, and it's time that the Church get a hold of this truth and watch the manifestation of hidden treasures come to light...If our eschatology is dismal with a chaotic conclusion, we will not arrest, access, and assess the nations for global destiny. Instead, our fear of the "[1]*end times*" as some would put it, will shape our thinking process towards Kingdom economy, and our focus will be aimed for a quick flight (rapture) out of this madness instead of the Meek inheriting the earth...

Isaiah 45:3

I will give you the treasures of darkness And hidden riches of secret places, That you may know that I, the LORD, *Who call you by your name, Am the God of Israel.*

I would love to reread this verse in **'my' translation**:

I will give you the treasures (depository, cellar, armory, storehouse) of darkness (stuff where you never thought it would come from, or

---

[1] For more on this see the author's book titled "Are We Living in The End Times or The Last Days?" You can source a copy here: https://www.amazon.com/Are-Living-Times-Final-Days/dp/1486623174 Or the eBook at: https://apostlemscantlebury.com/store/are-we-living-in-the-end-times-or-the-last-days

appear), and the hidden riches (secret storehouse, a secreted valuable, money, hid treasure) of secret places. (The coin in the fish's mouth, pocketbooks, wallets, bank accounts, policies, inheritances, investments, commodities, and most of all, things you could never fathom or imagine), that you may know that I, the Lord, Who call you by your name, Am the God of Israel.

Psalms 66:10-13

For you, O God, have proved us: you have tried us, as silver is tried. You brought us into the net; you laid affliction upon our loins. You have caused men to ride over our heads; we went through fire and through water: but you brought us out into a wealthy place. I will go into your house with burnt offerings: I will pay you my vows.

Wealth here is defined as satisfaction, abundance, and that which runs over and over.

Luke 6:38...*Pressed down, shaking together, and running over...*

The Lord is turning our captivity away and making us into people that trust Him for everything. Matthew 6:33 But seek you first (and foremost) the Kingdom of God, and his righteousness, and all of these things will be added unto you.

As we bring this section of teaching to a close, I would like for us to do something that I have never done before. Let us pray and rejoice together in the Lord of Provision and for the Provision of the Lord. Let us boldly and faithfully pray the following prayer together:

Father, In Jesus' Name, we thank You for the supernatural abundance, wealth, and prosperity of Your people, and the universal joy that shall resound throughout all of the earth just how generous, great and mighty You are. I thank You for the manifestation of the Spirit through Kingdom wealth, finance, and reformed Kingdom economics, and the converting of the wealth of this world over into the Saints of the Lord most high. IN ORDER to advance the Kingdom of God, and to meet the specific and strategic needs of Your people in Jesus' Name. We decree by the Spirit of the Lord, that wealth and prosperity shall spring forth in marvelous ways and means, confounding and breaking into pieces, even the very enemy and adversary thereof. In fact, we thank You that the enemy will have to surrender our goods, and bring them to our feet, for You said every knee shall bow, and every tongue shall confess that Jesus Christ is Lord to the glory of God. Therefore, we thank and praise Your Name for the fulfillment of Your word in the lives of Your people, and a new praise in the earth that will cause the glory of God to drop down like the rain as never before, to water the earth and Your precious people as it is becoming a TIDE of apostolic and prophetic events to transcend many generations, a memorial unto the Lord in Jesus' Name. To You be the glory and honor, dominion and power, in Jesus' Matchless Name! Amen and so be it!

In our next chapter I would like to climax this teaching on wealth and prosperity with some further thoughts and understanding.

LET'S CHECK OUR UNDERSTANDING OF CHAPTER 11—PRINCIPLES OF WEALTH AND PROSPERITY—THREE

1. Do you believe God is interested in our material wellbeing and is the provider of all good things? Explain with Scriptural backing.
2. According to Deuteronomy 8:17-18, what is the purpose for God granting us supernatural/divinely enabled wealth?
3. What is the Hebrew word translated "wealth" in 2 Chronicles 1:12? What does it literally mean?
4. What is it that God is shaping us to become through the length of time we spend in experiencing lack in material things (type of wilderness)?
5. How will developing meekness help us inherit the wealth that God had intended for us?
6. Why will our accurate understanding of the end times be of utmost importance in securing *"the treasures of darkness and hidden riches of secret places"* as stated in Isaiah 45:3?
7. Why is it important for us to trust Him in everything, in all aspects of our lives before He can release the hidden wealth into our hands?
8. What are the key Kingdom Principles for obtaining and using supernatural wealth that you have been able to glean from the author's prayer?

CHAPTER TWELVE
PRINCIPLES OF WEALTH AND PROSPERITY – FOUR

Isaiah 60 indicates that the Spirit quickens our hearts indeed, to the universal (let me break this word down for you: Uni—one, Verse—a sequence of words) truth, that one of God's ultimate intentions through the socio-economic realm is for the Saints to possess unprecedented wealth in the advancement of His Kingdom, and to also enjoy it faithfully in the Lord as we honour Him with our substance.

There is a divine shifting with new patterns developing in the Church for a new kind of faith and a new kind of harvest. Prophetically, it is perceived and is now being proclaimed that the supernatural wealth factor is being pioneered through a new breed of quality Saints, a people of Kingdom authority that has the mind of the Spirit to discern where these measures and treasures of prophetic prosperity is coming from, even to the speaking forth of these glorious dimensions for the full manifestation of wealth and Kingdom finance unto Kingdom advancement.

Though the prophetic may cause you to cross over Jordan to inherit the apostolic blessings, it is the apostolic dimension, which establishes and disburses this new interacting paradigm and dimensional shifting of unprecedented Kingdom wealth with the administration of present truth Apostles. Together with the Prophets, the Apostles are trailblazing a new dynamic in the corporate anointing to oversee this new wealth factor, which is being released through the Spirit of God for such a time as this. This new dimension of financial wealth shall usher in the glory of the

Lord throughout the ends of the earth and shall cause the nations to realize the true source of salvation, wealth, health, prosperity, and well-being, which is the Lord God Himself.

FROM INTERFERING TO TRANSFERRING

By reviewing Webster's New World Dictionary, I have discovered importantly that to proclaim the abundant harvest and inheritance of the corporate, Saints must consider the position they have in the Spirit, and the powerful force of that spiritual position.

Now, the negative idea of interfering is where many Saints are grossly preoccupied. For them, interference is the daily onslaught of countless many who would rather conclude that God's promises are Nay instead of Yeah! For them, the continuous struggle for deliverance, breakthrough, and blessing has become such a familiar thing, that daring to believe beyond the confines of frustrating struggles may seem a bit too far-fetched.

With whispering hopes that Heaven is the only real solution out of their hectic problems, many Saints **resort to what I would term "rapture-mania" and visions of "Beulah Land" (or Fantasy Island) as a means of escape from the subtle and overt attacks against their wealth preservation, or in truth, their position of the Spirit, the pre-ordained and pre-fixed revelation of God for their lives.**

Nevertheless, in all hopes of each Saint finding rest in the Lord in all things, I began to ponder a bit just how colossal and awesome God is in dealing with us.

Let's now seek to define the principles of both the Words "Interfering [interference] and transferring [transference]."

Interference has to do with the idea of **coming into collision or opposition with**. It has also to do with **coming in or between for some purpose, and to intervene**. If you are referring to Radio and Television, Sports (particularly Football or Hockey, even Basketball), Physics, and Patent Law, the term "Interference" carries differing aspects and shades of meaning as well.

Interference is not to be viewed from a negative disposition only, as if satan is gaining ground on what God has for you. But interfering can be a Sovereign intervention of the Lord Most High. Here, interfering can actually be God's way of baffling the minds of men through the unfathomable riches and resources of His Glory. It can simply mean that the Lord of Hosts is transcending and superseding finite and limited mentalities, bringing into manifestation, tangibility, and substance the creative and proceeding (OR NOW) Word of the Lord in the midst of those whom He chooses. Because not every detour or delay is demonic. At times it is God in His Sovereign will operating in our lives. For example: Acts 16:6-7

> *Now when they had gone through Phrygia and the region of Galatia, they were forbidden by the Holy Spirit to preach the word in Asia. After they had come to Mysia, they tried to go into Bithynia, but the Spirit did not permit them.*

As recorded in Isaiah 55:11

> *So shall my word be that goes forth* (proceeding word—Matthew 4:4; Romans 10:17; Ephesians 6:18—rhema, uttered, and quickening word) *out of my mouth. It shall not return unto me void, but will accomplish what I please; and shall prosper in the thing that I send it.* [Emphasis Author's]

Yes, in the purest sense, it is the Lord who is turning over the tables of men, to divinely accomplish His desired, intended, and decreed purpose from the beginning...

Isaiah 46:10

> *With God the Father, his counsel shall stand, and he will do all of his pleasure!*

Now, the word **"Transference"** is indeed a rather interesting word. However, to cover the basic definition and meaning of the word "Transference," let us look also at the word "Transfer." Here, the word "Transfer is defined primarily as **"To carry, convey, remove, or send from one person, place, or position to another."**

But the question revolving around your mind may be "What is this great transferring all about? What does it entail, and for what purpose?

Are we being divinely set up by God to receive an abundance of corporate release, unprecedented global wealth increase of the most colossal kind?

From the corporate standpoint, yes! God is actively increasing within His Church the unstoppable massive momentum of new millennium wealth for a new destiny. This transferring of wealth from Heaven and earth is more than just getting our needs met. It is bringing about a bold new witness to creation that God is truly a very good God, He is faithful to all generations, is generous and gratuitous in nature.

MENTALITIES BEING TRANSFORMED TO GOD'S KINGDOM WEALTH

The new wealth factor is spreading over the nations like a blanket from Heaven. It will cover the earth in awesome wonder, as the world system will bow its knee to the Most High God of the Most Holy Place. Angelic demonstration of the wealth harvest will become more evident in the affairs of the Saints, as multitudes of Saints will testify of the supernatural dimension of wealth and Kingdom resources in their bank accounts, and any other receptacle of expenditure or savings.

More and more, Saints abroad will discover their credit reports with a new twist. The Year of Jubilee, The Feast of Tabernacles, The Lord's Release, and the Acceptable Year of the Lord shall become a present truth reality to countless many on a very tangible level. The prison doors of old order mentalities will become unlocked to new realities of the Spirit. Billions and Trillions of dollars shall arise out of the sea of uncertainty and shall swim ashore to the land of doubly fruitful. For as it stands, there is enough wealth in the entire world that could end poverty for all people right now. Yes, there is enough wealth resources for every person on this planet to enjoy the good of the land, to have their homes paid off, vehicle, too, and to adapt a business plan to continuing the perpetual wealth factor in Kingdom designed to the betterment of their service one to another as unto the Lord. You can read these two chapters—Deuteronomy 8 and Deuteronomy 28,

Now understand, that money is but one part of the economy of God, the means to transfer, allot, and engage in legal venues of financial expression. However, when referring to wealth and money, one can't help but associate the two. Therefore, let us look at the distinctive meanings of both money and wealth.

Money is defined from the Webster's New World Dictionary as "Standard pieces of gold, silver, copper, nickel, etc., stamped by government authority and used as a medium of exchange and measure of value. Any paper note issued by a government or and authorized bank and used in the same way." Any substance or article can be used as money or exchange, including property (houses, land, automobiles, jewelry, etc.), possessions, accounts, timeshare, stocks, bank notes, precious metals, natural resources and checks. But again, money is only but one part of the matter as Kingdom wealth is the mentality or mindset that moves the money about.

WEALTH

Wealth does not merely begin or end with money, but wealth is a state of being and a way of LIFE. Money is important to circulate, but God is getting us into a new mentality that will shift money, and all other needed exchanges, into a new sphere and dimension of grace and glory with God. For the highest kind of wealth is GOD himself, he is the Source to our resource.

Wealth is an idea. In the Middle English definition of wealth, it carries the meaning of happiness. Wealth began as God's idea from Genesis 1:28. Man was given dominion over the earth, and as such all of its wealth and resources.

Wealth was God's idea from the start, as man was given a five-fold charge to be fruitful, multiply, replenish, subdue, and have dominion. Genesis 1, bears record of the first Great Commission of man. We like to call this the Dominion Mandate, for everything about God's dealings with man begins with Dominion, the King's Domain! It is the first Great Commission. Everything God is doing through the Church today points back to the original plan, design, intent, and purpose of God for man to have Kingdom dominion in the earth. Everything!

Therefore, one must define wealth from the standpoint that God is in control, and that we must view things as the Psalmist declared it: Psalm 24:1 *the earth is the Lord's and the fullness thereof, the world and they that dwell therein...* We could read the entire Psalm:

WEALTH THAT REFORMS THE CHURCH IS SO THAT IT CAN REFORM AND TRANSFORM THE NATIONS

Please allow me to share with you a vision I have for the global Church, the Body of Christ in the earth!

The Church needs to be brought into a new upward spiral and frequency of the Spirit to receive and administrate the abundance of grace God has for Her through wealth resource.

As an Apostle, along with many others across the globe in Apostolic diversity, there is a new perception and apprehension of the wealth transfer from the New Millennium leader-shift (21st Century preparation) into the Corporate Body of Christ, released through the Body to impact nations, and to change our world through dominion, the liberating influence of the King and His Kingdom.

There is coming to pass what I believe to be a colossal wealth resource of the most glorious kind that will cause even the world to recognize the Father God as their true source. Somehow, men the world over will discover their hidden genius and potential by observing the Saints at large coming into diversified wealth management and reformed Kingdom economics.

And I do believe that in a matter of time, businesses all over the world will begin to think differently about God, and the corporate glory of the Saints. Now, allow me to give you what I believe to be 8 great reasons as to why, the supernatural wealth shall saturate the Church. They are as follows...

1. The Spirit of the Lord is bringing a new paradigm and dimension of financial reformation and renewal to the Church to change the world. The world shall begin to see that it is the Saints of the Lord most High who is the true standard of the Kingdom community, not the government of the land. By moving our mindsets from Christian to King Priest, or from Church to Kingdom, we bring a whole new influence on the earth.

2. The Spirit of the Lord is causing the Saints to become responsible in financial matters. No more will the Saints at large decree in faith for the erasure of bad debt, which many have accrued through their own disappointing efforts. But the Lord is going to cause a new shift and pattern of events to transpire in the corporate Church,

and in the mindsets and mentalities of HIS people, to get the Saints to see that it is not only the need to ask in faith for closure of old debts, but to become better stewards itself...New ways and means of circulating and communicating wealth resources...

3. The Spirit of the Lord is causing a new sound to roar over the nations, as more businesses will develop covenant relationships with Apostles and Prophets. Prophets of the NOW configuration of the Kingdom are given the divine foresight and insight of where the wealth harvest is, but it is the Apostles of the Spirit with the Prophets, who will administer and execute this wealth strategy through the Church to the nations. As in Acts 4 and 5, the possessions, wealth, and provisions shall continue to be laid at the Apostles' feet.

4. The Spirit of the Lord is raining down a deluge of His glory to dispense to the Saints abroad the means to becoming good stewards in their personal life. More and more Saints will get their houses in order, and shall show forth as a witness to others that Believers can be trustworthy, honest, genuine, and true in their dealings one with another, even to those who profess not the Lord.

5. The Spirit of the Lord is causing a massive wave of transferred wealth to infuse the Church, and the Church shall infuse the world system with new territorial and global authority. The news reports shall keep the world abreast of the happenings of the Church, as the United Nations, the capitals of our nations, and the ruling governments of this world will look to find answers among the corporate Saints. We are speaking of global transformation...

6. The Spirit of the Lord shall cause the earth to tremble at the mention of the Saints. Daniel 7 confirms that the Saints are the ones who possess the Kingdom. Through Christ we shall fully possess the kingdoms of this world, and the heathen shall become our inheritance.

7. The Spirit of the Lord is causing a fire to burn in the midst of His Saints, as this reveals a new kind of witness and evangelization. This new evangelization shall ignite reformation fire, which shall spread over the nations. For the Lord who answers by fire shall cause many unbelievers to know Him through the stability of financial stewardship among the Saints. There shall arise a new breed

of evangelization from the reformation of wealth and finance. Barriers between poor and rich shall be broken down. Mammon shall bow its knee to the Lordship of Jesus Christ, as unbelievers shall witness the joy in serving God honestly with all of their heart and with all of their substance.

8. The Spirit of the Lord shall cause a New River to flow throughout the nations. Wealth shall abundantly increase in Third World nations. People all over the world shall see that their purpose attracts provision, and their destiny shall be fulfilled with the aid and support of exchangeable means to accomplish their given purpose. Unprecedented giving shall increase magnificently throughout the earth. The Body of Christ shall have more than enough to herald the gospel and advance the Kingdom abroad. Giving shall exceed the expectations of many Elders as the Church comes into divine order in giving and receiving, and in right relationships in vertical and horizontal ministries. This same pattern will affect change in our socio-economic infrastructure, bringing revolutionary and radical changes in all sectors of the nations. The oppressed shall be set free, and a new respect of God, His people, and one another shall reach into the vast Heavens. Giving shall become a way of living, and living shall be an expression of our heart in giving. Stinginess shall be no more but a whisper, a past fading, an old story of the unfolding of HIS glory...

SO, THEN WE NEED TO ARISE AND SHINE!

Isaiah 60:1-5, 11

Arise and shine, for your light has come, and the glory of the Lord has risen upon you. For behold the darkness shall cover the earth, and gross darkness the people. But the Lord shall arise upon you, and his glory shall be seen upon you. And the Gentiles shall come to your light, and kings to the brightness of your rising. Lift up your eyes round about, and see: all gather themselves together: they come to you: your sons shall come from afar, and your daughters shall be nursed at your side. Then you shall see, and flow together, and your heart shall fear and be enlarged: because the abundance of the sea shall be converted unto you. The wealth of the nations shall come to you.

Therefore your gates shall be open continually. They shall not be shut day or night, that men may bring unto you the wealth of the nations...

So, as we begin closing this series on Wealth and Finance let me declare this Apostolic Blessing over us:

Let us feed the seed and nurture the nature for by divine enlightenment we are becoming what we already are in Christ Jesus, our Lord...

In the next chapter of this book, we would look at the significance of first fruits.

LET'S CHECK OUR UNDERSTANDING OF CHAPTER 12: PRINCIPLES OF WEALTH AND PROSPERITY—FOUR

1. What is your understanding of Isaiah 60?
2. Do you agree with the author's statement "There is a divine shifting with new patterns developing in the Church for a new kind of faith and a new kind of harvest." Explain
3. Who could be considered **quality Saints** according to the author? Fill in the Blanks:
   The p_ _ _ _ _ _ _c may cause you to c_ _ _s over J_ _ _ _ n to i_ _ _ _ _t the apostolic blessings, it is the apostolic d_ _ _ _ _ _ _n, which e_ _ _ _ _ _ _ _ _s and d_ _ _ _ _ _ _s this new interacting paradigm and dimensional s_ _ _ _ _ _g of unprecedented K_ _ _ _ _m w_ _ _ _h with the administration of p_ _ _ _ _t truth Apostles.
4. Why do you believe many Saints are unable to believe God for beyond the confines of frustrating struggles for deliverance and breakthrough?
5. How does the author mean by "rapture-mania" and visions of "Beulah Land"?
6. How prevalent are these mentalities among the Christian communities around you?
7. Why should we not view interference only from a negative perspective?

8. Are you witnessing the transferring process taking place in corporate Christian communities?
9. How excited are you to be a part of this great "Year of Jubilee" time period?
10. What is the distinctive difference between money and wealth?
11. What is the purpose for God to pour out supernatural wealth upon His corporate body globally?
12. What are the reasons for God saturating the corporate body of Saints with supernatural wealth?
13. As Isaiah 60:1-5,11 aptly states, what is expected of His corporate Body and us as individuals as He releases this wealth into our lives?

Chapter Thirteen
Understanding the Significance of Firstfruits

FIRSTFRUITS: THAT WHICH MATURES EARLY; THE CHOICE PART; THE TITHE.

KEY SCRIPTURES:

Exodus 23:16-17

and the Feast of Harvest, the firstfruits of your labors which you have sown in the field; and the Feast of Ingathering at the end of the year, when you have gathered in the fruit of your labors from the field. "Three times in the year all your males shall appear before the Lord God.

Leviticus 23:9-22

And the Lord spoke to Moses, saying, "Speak to the children of Israel, and say to them: 'When you come into the land which I give to you, and reap its harvest, then you shall bring a sheaf of the firstfruits of your harvest to the priest. He shall wave the sheaf before the Lord, to be accepted on your behalf; on the day after the Sabbath the priest shall wave it. And you shall offer on that day, when you wave the sheaf, a male lamb of the first year, without blemish, as *a burnt offering to the LORD. Its grain offering shall be two-tenths of an ephah of fine flour mixed with oil, an offering made by fire to the LORD, for a sweet aroma; and its drink offering shall be of wine, one-fourth of a hin. You shall eat neither bread nor parched grain nor fresh grain until the same day that you have brought an offering to your God; it shall be a statute forever throughout your generations in all your dwellings. 'And you shall count for yourselves from the day after the Sabbath, from the day that you brought the sheaf of the wave offering: seven Sabbaths shall be completed. Count fifty days to the day after the seventh Sabbath; then you shall offer a new grain offering to the LORD. You shall bring from your dwellings two wave loaves of two-tenths of an ephah. They shall be of fine flour; they shall be baked with leaven. They are the firstfruits to the LORD. And you shall offer with the bread seven lambs of the first year, without blemish, one young bull, and two rams. They shall be as a burnt offering to the LORD, with their grain offering and their drink offerings, an offering made by fire for a sweet aroma to the LORD. Then you shall sacrifice one kid of the goats as a sin offering, and two male lambs of the first year as a sacrifice of a peace offering. The priest shall wave them with the bread of the firstfruits as a wave offering before the LORD, with the two lambs. They shall be holy to the LORD for the priest. And you shall proclaim on the same day that it is a holy convocation to you. You shall do no customary work on it. It shall be a statute forever in all your dwellings throughout your generations 'When you reap the harvest of your land, you shall not wholly reap the corners of your field when you reap, nor shall you gather any gleaning from your harvest. You shall leave them for the poor and for the stranger: I am the LORD your God.'*

Proverbs 3:9

Honor the LORD with your possessions, And with the firstfruits of all your increase.

Romans 8:23

Not only that, but we also who have the firstfruits of the Spirit, even we ourselves groan within ourselves, eagerly waiting for the adoption, the redemption of our body.

1 Corinthians 15:20

But now Christ is risen from the dead and has become the firstfruits of those who have fallen asleep.

FOUNDATIONAL INFORMATION:
The firstfruits is the firstborn of the flocks or the first vegetables and grains to be gathered at harvest time, thought of as belonging to God in a special sense. "Firstfruits" is from the Hebrew "bikkuwr" (Strong's #1061) which means "the first-fruits of the crop," as well as "beginning, first, choicest." Its root "bakar" (Strong's #1069) means "to burst the womb, (causatively) bear or make early fruit (of woman or tree)." Compare "re'shiyth" (Strong's #7225) which means "the first, in place, time, order or rank (specifically, a firstfruit)." Its root is "ro'sh," the Hebrew word for "head."

FULFILLED IN CHRIST:
Jesus Christ is the "Head" of the Church (Ephesians 1:23; 5:22),

which is His body, the fullness of Him who fills all in all.

Wives, submit to your own husbands, as to the Lord.

The "firstfruits" of them that slept (1 Corinthians 15:20).

But now Christ is risen from the dead and has become the firstfruits of those who have fallen asleep.

John revealed Him as the "beginning" ("chief") of the new creation (Revelation 3:14).

> *And to the angel of the church of the Laodiceans write, 'These things says the Amen, the Faithful and True Witness, the Beginning of the creation of God:*

Our risen King is the antitype of the Old Testament "sheaf of the firstfruits" (Leviticus 23:9-14)—this representative sheaf was a "forerunner" sheaf (Hebrews 6:19-20).

> *And the LORD spoke to Moses, saying, "Speak to the children of Israel, and say to them: 'When you come into the land which I give to you, and reap its harvest, then you shall bring a sheaf of the firstfruits of your harvest to the priest. He shall wave the sheaf before the LORD, to be accepted on your behalf; on the day after the Sabbath the priest shall wave it. And you shall offer on that day, when you wave the sheaf, a male lamb of the first year, without blemish, as a burnt offering to the LORD. Its grain offering shall be two-tenths of an ephah of fine flour mixed with oil, an offering made by fire to the LORD, for a sweet aroma; and its drink offering shall be of wine, one-fourth of a hin. You shall eat neither bread nor parched grain nor fresh grain until the same day that you have brought an offering to your God; it shall be a statute forever throughout your generations in all your dwellings.*

Hebrews 6:19-20

> *This hope we have as an anchor of the soul, both sure and steadfast, and which enters the Presence behind the veil, where the forerunner has entered for us, even Jesus, having become High Priest forever according to the order of Melchizedek.*

It was waved before the Father in His resurrection and ascension; Jesus was accepted for us (John 20:16-17; Ephesians 1:6-7).

The Father gave His "best" when He gave Jesus (Numbers 18:12 with John 3:16).

Our Savior is the "choice vine" (Genesis 49:11; compare John 15:1-5).

The Apostle Peter described His Lord as "a living stone, disallowed indeed of men, but chosen of God, and precious" (1 Peter 2:4).

APPLIED TO THE CHRISTIAN:
The Church is a called-out people for His name, the firstfruits of His creation (Acts 15:14-18).

The term "firstfruits" also speaks of the resurrection power of the new creation manifested as Believers arise to walk in newness of life (Romans 6:4).

After the resurrection of Jesus (as recorded in the Book of Acts), 120, then 3,000, then 5,000 soon followed their heavenly Head and passed from death unto life (John 5:24; Colossians 1:9-13).

The term "firstfruits" is particular to the Old Testament Feast of Pentecost (Exodus 23:16-17; Leviticus 23:15-22)—this New Testament experience was described by Paul as the "firstfruits" of the Spirit and the "earnest" of our inheritance (Romans 8:23; Ephesians 1:13-14).

Believers are to tithe their substance (Malachi 3:8-12), bringing unto the Lord the "firstfruits" of all our increase (Proverbs 3:9).

In the book of Revelation we read about God's "last days" Church going to be full of overcomers, the "firstfruits" unto God and the Lamb (Revelation 14:1-5).

And We Could Go Deeper: Let us briefly look at the following:

Exodus 23:19; 34:22, 26

The first of the firstfruits of your land you shall bring into the house of the LORD your God. You shall not boil a young goat in its mother's milk.

And you shall observe the Feast of Weeks, of the firstfruits of wheat harvest, and the Feast of Ingathering at the year's end.

"The first of the firstfruits of your land you shall bring to the house of the LORD your God. You shall not boil a young goat in its mother's milk."

Leviticus 2:12-14

As for the offering of the firstfruits, you shall offer them to the LORD, but they shall not be burned on the altar for a sweet aroma.

And every offering of your grain offering you shall season with salt; you shall not allow the salt of the covenant of your God to be lacking from your grain offering. With all your offerings you shall offer salt. 'If you offer a grain offering of your firstfruits to the Lord, you shall offer for the grain offering of your firstfruits green heads of grain roasted on the fire, grain beaten from full heads.

Numbers 28:26

Also on the day of the firstfruits, when you bring a new grain offering to the Lord at your Feast of Weeks, you shall have a holy convocation. You shall do no customary work.

Deuteronomy 12:11; 18:4; 26:10

then there will be the place where the Lord your God chooses to make His name abide. There you shall bring all that I command you: your burnt offerings, your sacrifices, your tithes, the heave offerings of your hand, and all your choice offerings which you vow to the Lord.

The firstfruits of your grain and your new wine and your oil, and the first of the fleece of your sheep, you shall give him.

and now, behold, I have brought the firstfruits of the land which you, O Lord, have given me.' "Then you shall set it before the Lord your God, and worship before the Lord your God.

1 Samuel 9:2

And he had a choice and handsome son whose name was Saul. There was not a more handsome person than he among the children of Israel. From his shoulders upward he was taller than any of the people.

Chapter Thirteen: Understanding the Significance of Firstfruits

2 Samuel 10:9

When Joab saw that the battle line was against him before and behind, he chose some of Israel's best and put them in battle array against the Syrians.

2 Kings 4:42; 19:23

Then a man came from Baal Shalisha and brought the man of God bread of the firstfruits, twenty loaves of barley bread, and newly ripened grain in his knapsack. And he said, "Give it to the people, that they may eat.

By your messengers you have reproached the Lord, And said: "By the multitude of my chariots I have come up to the height of the mountains, To the limits of Lebanon; I will cut down its tall cedars And its choice cypress trees; I will enter the extremity of its borders, To its fruitful forest.

1 Chron: 7:40; 19:10

All these were the children of Asher, heads of their fathers' houses, choice men, mighty men of valor, chief leaders. And they were recorded by genealogies among the army fit for battle; their number was twenty-six thousand.

When Joab saw that the battle line was against him before and behind, he chose some of Israel's best and put them in battle array against the Syrians.

2 Chron: 25:5; 31:5

Moreover Amaziah gathered Judah together and set over them captains of thousands and captains of hundreds, according to their fathers' houses, throughout all Judah and Benjamin; and he numbered them from twenty years old and above, and found them to be three hundred thousand choice men, able to go to war, who could handle spear and shield.

As soon as the commandment was circulated, the children of Israel brought in abundance the firstfruits of grain and wine, oil and honey, and of all the produce of the field; and they brought in abundantly the tithe of everything.

Nehemiah 10:35-37; 12:44; 13:31

And we made ordinances to bring the firstfruits of our ground and the firstfruits of all fruit of all trees, year by year, to the house of the LORD; to bring the firstborn of our sons and our cattle, as it is written in the Law, and the firstborn of our herds and our flocks, to the house of our God, to the priests who minister in the house of our God; to bring the firstfruits of our dough, our offerings, the fruit from all kinds of trees, the new wine and oil, to the priests, to the storerooms of the house of our God; and to bring the tithes of our land to the Levites, for the Levites should receive the tithes in all our farming communities.

And at the same time some were appointed over the rooms of the storehouse for the offerings, the firstfruits, and the tithes, to gather into them from the fields of the cities the portions specified by the Law for the priests and Levites; for Judah rejoiced over the priests and Levites who ministered.

and to bringing the wood offering and the firstfruits at appointed times.

Proverbs 8:10, 19

Receive my instruction, and not silver, And knowledge rather than choice gold;

My fruit is better than gold, yes, than fine gold, And my revenue than choice silver.

Song of Solomon 6:9

My dove, my perfect one, Is the only one, The only one of her mother, The favorite of the one who bore her. The daughters saw her And called her blessed, The queens and the concubines, And they praised her.

Jeremiah 2:3

Israel was holiness to the LORD, The firstfruits of His increase. All that devour him will offend; Disaster will come upon them," says the LORD.'

Ezekiel 20:40; 44:30; 48:14

For on My holy mountain, on the mountain height of Israel," says the Lord GOD, "there all the house of Israel, all of them in the land, shall serve Me; there I will accept them, and there I will require your offerings and the firstfruits of your sacrifices, together with all your holy things.

The best of all firstfruits of any kind, and every sacrifice of any kind from all your sacrifices, shall be the priest's; also you shall give to the priest the first of your ground meal, to cause a blessing to rest on your house.

And they shall not sell or exchange any of it; they may not alienate this best part of the land, for it is holy to the LORD.

Romans 11:16; 16:5

For if the firstfruit is holy, the lump is also holy; and if the root is holy, so are the branches.

Likewise greet the church that is in their house. Greet my beloved Epaenetus, who is the firstfruits of Achaia to Christ.

1 Corinthians 15:23; 16:15

But each one in his own order: Christ the firstfruits, afterward those who are Christ's at His coming.

I urge you, brethren—you know the household of Stephanas, that it is the firstfruits of Achaia, and that they have devoted themselves to the ministry of the saints

James 1:18

Of His own will He brought us forth by the word of truth, that we might be a kind of firstfruits of His creatures.

In our final chapter we would be taking a deeper look at mammon.

LET'S CHECK OUR UNDERSTANDING OF CHAPTER 13: UNDERSTANDING THE SIGNIFICANCE OF FIRSTFRUITS

1. What is the Hebrew word translated "Firstfruits" and what does this literally mean?
2. What is the meaning of the Hebrew word "re'shiyth"? Where in the Bible is this word used and in what context?
3. Our r_ _ _ n King is the antitype of the Old Testament s_ _ _f pf the f_ _ _ _ _ _ _ _s. This representative sheaf was a f_ _ _ _ _ _ _r.
4. According to Hebrews 6:19-20 what die Jesus Christ the forerunner achieve for us?
5. How does the "Church" the called-out people of God fit into the description of "firstfruits"?
6. What is the significance of the "firstfruits", tithes and offerings to the present-day Believer?

CHAPTER FOURTEEN
ANOTHER VIEW OF MAMMON

MATTHEW 6:24

No one can serve two masters; for either he will hate the one and love the other, or else he will be loyal to the one and despise the other. You cannot serve God and **mammon**. [Emphasis Author's]

[2]MAMMON – CAN ALSO BE DEFINED AS THE TREASURE PEOPLE TRUST IN (WHENever people's treasures are elsewhere other than in God or in a different sphere, it was referred to as mammon). Mammon is of Chaldean origin (confidence, i.e. wealth, personified); mammon's definition: riches. Usage: (Aramaic), riches, money, possessions, property. i.e. avarice (deified)—mammon. In the context of the verse Jesus said what one finds confidence in, and establish relations with, they then use to their advantage.

Now, whenever God calls a man, the first level of temptation he would have to deal with is always mammon. Mammon appeals to unaddressed flesh and always configures its conversation to the type and quality of the assignment/mandate one is given. Mammon competes for an assignment and recruits you for that same assignment. However, it seeks to function for "team dark" or the dark realm, because it always offers you a shortcut

---

[2] This chapter is adapted from a teaching by Apostle Brandon Bailey of Teleios, South Africa. And used by permission.

to what God already promised and guaranteed you. Let us consider a few times when mammon spoke:

Matthew 4:8-9

Again, the devil took Him up on an exceedingly high mountain and showed Him all the kingdoms of the world and their glory. And he said to Him, "All these things I will give You if You will fall down and worship me."

Genesis 3:1-5

Now the serpent was more cunning than any beast of the field which the LORD God had made. And he said to the woman, "Has God indeed said, 'You shall not eat of every tree of the garden'?" And the woman said to the serpent, "We may eat the fruit of the trees of the garden; but of the fruit of the tree which is in the midst of the garden, God has said, 'You shall not eat it, nor shall you touch it, lest you die.' " Then the serpent said to the woman, "You will not surely die. For God knows that in the day you eat of it your eyes will be opened, and you will be like God, knowing good and evil."

Matthew 26:6-16

And when Jesus was in Bethany at the house of Simon the leper, a woman came to Him having an alabaster flask of very costly fragrant oil, and she poured it on His head as He sat at the table. But when His disciples saw it, they were indignant, saying, "Why this waste? For this fragrant oil might have been sold for much and given to the poor." But when Jesus was aware of it, He said to them, "Why do you trouble the woman? For she has done a good work for Me. For you have the poor with you always, but Me you do not have always. For in pouring this fragrant oil on My body, she did it for My burial. Assuredly, I say to you, wherever this gospel is preached in the whole world, what this woman has done will also be told as a memorial to her." Then one of the twelve, called Judas Iscariot, went to the chief priests and said, "What are you willing to give me if I deliver Him to you?" And they counted out to him thirty pieces of silver. So, from that time he sought opportunity to betray Him.

SOMETHING TO NOTE:
Mammon appeals to areas of doubt and insecurities. The areas in our lives where we doubt ourselves the most becomes a default entry for mammon to appeal to us. It becomes a FALSE COVER UP FOR AREAS, where the Holy Spirit WANTS TO CONFRONT AND HEAL. It provides a false seal and covering for the things that God wants to address through the processing of His Word and His Holy Spirit.

For Judas—lack and shortage of money made him feel inferior and that became the default entry for satan through mammon. Let us look at this a bit deeper. Let us begin where the process starts, when this lady blessed Jesus with expensive ointment (Matthew 26:7) and what Judas felt he deserved became the default entry for mammon into his life. See John 13:26-27

Jesus answered, "It is he to whom I shall give a piece of bread when I have dipped it." And having dipped the bread, He gave it to Judas Iscariot, the son of Simon. Now after the piece of bread, Satan entered him. Then Jesus said to him, "What you do, do quickly."

For Eve—satan fed her insecurities and made her doubt herself and made her doubt what God said and offered her a way to address those doubts and insecurities. That became the default entry for a type of mammon into her life.

For Jesus, the kingdoms of this world were His inheritance, but satan wanted to give Him reward without process and tried to appeal to what he considered doubts/insecurities and offered a way out. See Matthew 4:8-11

Again, the devil took Him up on an exceedingly high mountain and showed Him all the kingdoms of the world and their glory. And he said to Him, "All these things I will give You if You will fall down and worship me." Then Jesus said to him, "Away with you, Satan! For it is written, 'You shall worship the LORD your God, and Him only you shall serve.'" Then the devil left Him, and behold, angels came and ministered to Him.

Daniel 2:44

And in the days of these kings the God of heaven will set up a kingdom which shall never be destroyed; and the kingdom shall not be left to other people; it shall break in pieces and consume all these kingdoms, and it shall stand forever.

Daniel 7:14

Then to Him was given dominion and glory and a kingdom, that all peoples, nations, and languages should serve Him. His dominion is an everlasting dominion, which shall not pass away, And His kingdom the one Which shall not be destroyed.

In this context we now begin to understand the broadness of mammon's reach, because mammon does not merely provide money, but mammon provides:

- Status/Rank
- Influence
- Power
- Platform

Mammon's strategy of recruitment is human insecurity, and it appeals to the things that men believe makes them inferior to other men. Men who have wrestled for years with their own sense of doubt, insecurity, and fear tend to address that and they tend to become extremist and bullies once they get these things.

The dark realm in which mammon functions exalts us without building humility in us. On the other hand, God exalts us after building humility in us and that is very necessary to address the potential power mammon might have on us in the future. God's process purges us of false ambitions and contextualises the assignment in such a way that we understand: The POWER, THE GLORY and The KINGDOM belongs to God and not us.

Now our insecurities, our fears and our doubts do not always go away but God's Spirit processes us to the extent that it does not hinder our assignment. satan on the other hand gives us a faulty cover up and we use rank, influence, power and platform to overcompensate for what is inherently weak in us.

When we are bound by an inferiority complex we don't fix it with rank, influence, platform and power, we fix it with repentance and reject the idea that we are less than who God says we are, and we allow the call of God to recalibrate us to the extent that we shift our confession and say what God says not what our inherent challenges say. This is how Paul addresses the thin veil between an inferiority complex and a superiority complex: 2 Corinthians 12:9

And He said to me, "My grace is sufficient for you, for My strength is made perfect in weakness." Therefore most gladly I will rather boast in my infirmities, that the power of Christ may rest upon me.

Jesus frames the relationship with mammon and God: Matthew 6:24

No one can serve two masters; for either he will hate the one and love the other, or else he will be loyal to the one and despise the other. You cannot serve God and mammon.

The relationship is framed with two clear words: masters and servants, let us explore these two words:

The word master and the word Lord was used interchangeably in the Scriptures:

The word Lord comes from the Greek word Kurios—koo'-ree-os
It is a noun and is masculine
NAS (National Academy of Sciences) Word Usage

1. He to whom a person or thing belongs, about which he has the power of deciding; master, lord. The possessor and disposer of a thing.
    1. The owner; one who has control of the person, the master.
    2. In the state: the sovereign, prince, chief, the Roman emperor.

2. Is a title of honour expressive of respect and reverence, with which servants greet their master.
3. This title is given to God, the Messiah!

The following verse captures it so well: Matthew 8:9

For I also am a man under authority, having soldiers under me. And I say to this one, 'Go,' and he goes; and to another, 'Come,' and he comes; and to my servant, 'Do this,' and he does it.

So, the end goal of mammon is control and that control is often facilitated through a dogma. Every system of control has a dogma. Dogma can be defined as a set of principles that govern and control how things are done under that umbrella. Jesus frames the agenda of mammon and He uses a very distinct word when He says:

"No one can serve two masters", masters have agendas and those agendas employ servants who are not allowed to preserve and protect their identity but have to adopt the identity of their master. See Genesis 17:27 NIV

And every male in Abraham's household, including those born in his household or bought from a foreigner, was circumcised with him.

Revelation 13:16-17 NIV

It also forced all people, great and small, rich and poor, free and slave, to receive a mark on their right hands or on their foreheads, so that they could not buy or sell unless they had the mark, which is the name of the beast or the number of its name.

Notice the mark of the servants allows it to transact within the system at the expense of identity and authenticity. To become a servant of the system creates a transactional benefit but you must be willing to surrender your authenticity.

Now this is where Jesus used the words "What will it profit a man to gain the world and to lose his soul"

The word soul comes from the word "psuche" and it is what makes a person distinct. In the context of Scripture, it is the breath of God that enters a person that makes him a conscious being who can think, who can reason, who can discern and who can judge.

Mammon contends for that and in exchange for the soul gives:

- Status/Rank
- Influence
- Power
- Platform

Mammon is operative in any individual who can reward you with the above and that person will force you to suspend your ability to reason as you serve out its agenda. A control freak administers mammon to the insecure and the doubtful. So even someone who genuinely loves God can default into mammon and administer it to control people who are battling with their insecurities, fears and doubts.

What mammon does when administered from the top:

It hides truth and perpetuates fallacies to win trust and eventually gain control of a person. The person then transacts with rank, influence, power and platform but has no position, no perspective, no opinion, no viewpoint and adopts the views of its master. This then perpetuates the agenda of mammon on a larger scale and the victims of mammon become desensitised to truth because self-preservation is more important than the liberty of the soul.

The strength of mammon is creating a false narrative of love when it simply feeds the lust for rank, influence, power and platform. Love amplifies identity, lust feeds the obsession with power, platform, influence and rank. The cost of it all is a change in who you are.

This leads to a diminished self identity and robs the individual of sound judgment so much so that the individual begins to believe [s]he is the persona that mammon created for him/her: Daniel 4:29-33

At the end of the twelve months, he was walking about the royal palace of Babylon. The king spoke, saying, "Is not this great Babylon, that I have built for a royal dwelling by my mighty power and for the honor of my majesty?" While the word was still in the king's mouth, a voice fell from heaven: "King Nebuchadnezzar, to you it is spoken: the kingdom has departed from you! And they shall drive you from men, and your dwelling shall be with the beasts of the field. They shall make you eat grass like oxen; and seven times shall pass over you, until you know that the Most High rules in the kingdom of men, and gives it to whomever He chooses." That very hour the word was fulfilled concerning Nebuchadnezzar; he was driven from men and ate grass like oxen; his body was wet with the dew of heaven till his hair had grown like eagles' feathers and his nails like birds' claws.

Acts 12:21-23

So on a set day Herod, arrayed in royal apparel, sat on his throne and gave an oration to them. And the people kept shouting, "The voice of a god and not of a man!" Then immediately an angel of the Lord struck him because he did not give glory to God. And he was eaten by worms and died.

Both kings had empires that covered up their fears and doubts and that became their default mammon that made them great amongst men. The success of the system and the success within the system gave them a persona they began to believe and that suffered the fate of their actions.

Now notice when mammon appeals to Paul and Barnabas trying to sell them a persona: Acts 14:8-18

And in Lystra a certain man without strength in his feet was sitting, a cripple from his mother's womb, who had never walked. This man heard Paul speaking. Paul, observing him intently and seeing that he had faith to be healed, said with a loud voice, "Stand up straight on your feet!" And he leaped and walked. Now when the people saw what Paul had done, they raised their voices, saying in the Lycaonian language, "The gods have come down to us in the likeness of men!" And Barnabas they called Zeus, and Paul, Hermes, because he was the chief speaker. Then the priest of Zeus, whose temple was in front of their city, brought oxen and garlands to the gates, intending to sacrifice with the multitudes. But when the apostles Barnabas and

Paul heard this, they tore their clothes and ran in among the multitude, crying out and saying, "Men, why are you doing these things? We also are men with the same nature as you, and preach to you that you should turn from these useless things to the living God, who made the heaven, the earth, the sea, and all things that are in them, who in bygone generations allowed all nations to walk in their own ways. Nevertheless He did not leave Himself without witness, in that He did good, gave us rain from heaven and fruitful seasons, filling our hearts with food and gladness." And with these sayings they could scarcely restrain the multitudes from sacrificing to them.

Now mammon develops personas and turns us like puppets on a string, and this is done when mammon rewards us with:

- Rank/Status
- Platform
- Influence
- Power

It dictates what flows from us and the content that flows from us is never coincidental but it is
well scripted and it is repeated over a period of time until the masses become desensitized and the abnormality is normalized because it is chosen, as long as it shapes the culture of the day. Mammon pays you to preach its narrative.

Every industry copy God and the premise by which God operates the consumption of the scroll. The scroll signifies God's dogma and God's agenda and informs how people should operate and function, mammon copies this methodology: Ezekiel 3:1-6

Moreover He said to me, "Son of man, eat what you find; eat this scroll, and go, speak to the house of Israel." So I opened my mouth, and He caused me to eat that scroll. And He said to me, "Son of man, feed your belly, and fill your stomach with this scroll that I give you." So I ate, and it was in my mouth like honey in sweetness. Then He said to me: "Son of man, go to the house of Israel and speak with My words to them. For you are not sent to a people of unfamiliar speech and of hard language, but to the house of Israel, not to many people of unfamiliar speech and of hard language, whose words you cannot understand. Surely, had I sent you to them, they would have listened to you.

Eat the scroll should be read in conjunction with: John 7:37-39

On the last day, that great day of the feast, Jesus stood and cried out, saying, "If anyone thirsts, let him come to Me and drink. He who believes in Me, as the Scripture has said, out of his heart will flow rivers of living water." But this He spoke concerning the Spirit, whom those believing in Him would receive; for the Holy Spirit was not yet given, because Jesus was not yet glorified.

Philippians 3:17-20

Brethren, join in following my example, and note those who so walk, as you have us for a pattern. For many walk, of whom I have told you often, and now tell you even weeping, that they are the enemies of the cross of Christ: whose end is destruction, whose god is their belly, and whose glory is in their shame—who set their mind on earthly things. For our citizenship is in heaven, from which we also eagerly wait for the Savior, the Lord Jesus Christ,

Consumption controls narrative is linked to the belly because the belly speaks to appetite, in this context our appetite for:

- Popularity
- Validation
- Acceptance
- Celebration

That appetite speaks the narrative of whoever meets its needs such as is found in Numbers 22:1-7

Then the children of Israel moved, and camped in the plains of Moab on the side of the Jordan across from Jericho. Now Balak the son of

Chapter Fourteen: Another View of Mammon

Zippor saw all that Israel had done to the Amorites. And Moab was exceedingly afraid of the people because they were many, and Moab was sick with dread because of the children of Israel. So Moab said to the elders of Midian, "Now this company will lick up everything around us, as an ox licks up the grass of the field." And Balak the son of Zippor was king of the Moabites at that time. Then he sent messengers to Balaam the son of Beor at Pethor, which is near the River in the land of the sons of his people, to call him, saying: "Look, a people has come from Egypt. See, they cover the face of the earth, and are settling next to me! Therefore please come at once, curse this people for me, for they are too mighty for me. Perhaps I shall be able to defeat them and drive them out of the land, for I know that he whom you bless is blessed, and he whom you curse is cursed." So the elders of Moab and the elders of Midian departed with the diviner's fee in their hand, and they came to Balaam and spoke to him the words of Balak.

Mammon paid him for his services to serve their agenda: 1 Kings 22:10-14

The king of Israel and Jehoshaphat the king of Judah, having put on their robes, sat each on his throne, at a threshing floor at the entrance of the gate of Samaria; and all the prophets prophesied before them. Now Zedekiah the son of Chenaanah had made horns of iron for himself; and he said, "Thus says the LORD: 'With these you shall gore the Syrians until they are destroyed.'" And all the prophets prophesied so, saying, "Go up to Ramoth Gilead and prosper, for the LORD will deliver it into the king's hand." Then the messenger who had gone to call Micaiah spoke to him, saying, "Now listen, the words of the prophets with one accord encourage the king. Please, let your word be like the word of one of them, and speak encouragement." And Micaiah said, "As the LORD lives, whatever the LORD says to me, that I will speak."

Now, I want you to notice that their belly was their God and shaped their narrative.

Mammon feeds the appetites of men and controls men like a puppet on a string to preach, promote and sell its agenda.

Culture is a reflection of:

- Values
- Beliefs
- Traditions

All of those combined become best practice to people and mammon gives its messengers the following: Rank, Platform, Power and Influence. In turn the messengers who have their belly as their god perpetuate this narrative because it has to reciprocate to the system and this becomes a perverse exchange and a perpetual cycle of give and take.

This is why the ascent into the Kingdom always starts with addressing appetites (god of the belly); God will take you through a harsh journey until the things that you think are very much a part of your life will fall away and you will no longer be forced to carry that weight and influence on you and then He gives the correct ways of God and Him alone to you.

Luke 22:31-32

And the Lord said, "Simon, Simon! Indeed, Satan has asked for you, that he may sift you as wheat. But I have prayed for you, that your faith should not fail; and when you have returned to Me, strengthen your brethren."

The process of sifting was to separate wheat from chaff, to separate the good from the bad. In the context of the verse, it is to separate that which belongs to God from that which belongs to mammon. In other words, satan believes he has a residue in you and it is his legitimate right to search for it in you.

Jesus speaks about this in John 14:30

I will no longer talk much with you, for the ruler of this world is coming, and he has nothing in Me.

The rewards of mammon can only be preserved with perversion.

Chapter Fourteen: Another View of Mammon

1 Kings 22:1-6

Now three years passed without war between Syria and Israel. Then it came to pass, in the third year, that Jehoshaphat the king of Judah went down to visit the king of Israel. And the king of Israel said to his servants, "Do you know that Ramoth in Gilead is ours, but we hesitate to take it out of the hand of the king of Syria?" So he said to Jehoshaphat, "Will you go with me to fight at Ramoth Gilead?" Jehoshaphat said to the king of Israel, "I am as you are, my people as your people, my horses as your horses." Also Jehoshaphat said to the king of Israel, "Please inquire for the word of the LORD today." Then the king of Israel gathered the prophets together, about four hundred men, and said to them, "Shall I go against Ramoth Gilead to fight, or shall I refrain?" So they said, "Go up, for the Lord will deliver it into the hand of the king."

Ahab supplies them with a platform and gives them influence but in order to preserve and protect their platform and influence, they have to prophesy favourably. That is a form of perversion. The root word for perversion is the word pervert. This word comes from the Greek word "metastrepho" and it means to change the purpose of something, to corrupt God's intention and expression. This definition suggests that anytime purpose and correct expression are lost we are dealing with a form of perversion. The goal of satan is to pervert purpose and to corrupt expression. Perversion makes us lose the integrity and the purity of the expression. In the verse above they lose the integrity and purity of the prophetic.

Mammon corrupts the person, and that corruption leads to a perverted expression:

The gift is perverted because the primary objective is self-preservation.

Another example where the gift and the rank is perverted: 1 Kings 13:1-30

And behold, a man of God went from Judah to Bethel by the word of the LORD, and Jeroboam stood by the altar to burn incense. Then he cried out against the altar by the word of the LORD, and said, "O altar, altar! Thus says the LORD: 'Behold, a child, Josiah by name, shall be born to the house of David; and on you he shall sacrifice the priests of the high places who burn incense on you, and men's bones shall be burned on you.'" And he gave a sign the same day, saying, "This is the sign which the Lord has spoken: Surely the altar shall split apart, and the ashes on it shall be poured out." So it came to pass when King Jeroboam heard the saying of the man of God, who cried out against the altar in Bethel, that he stretched out his hand from the altar, saying, "Arrest him!" Then his hand, which he stretched out toward him, withered, so that he could not pull it back to himself. The altar also was split apart, and the ashes poured out from the altar, according to the sign which the man of God had given by the word of the Lord. Then the king answered and said to the man of God, "Please entreat the favor of the Lord your God, and pray for me, that my hand may be restored to me." So the man of God entreated the Lord, and the king's hand was restored to him, and became as before. Then the king said to the man of God, "Come home with me and refresh yourself, and I will give you a reward." But the man of God said to the king, "If you were to give me half your house, I would not go in with you; nor would I eat bread nor drink water in this place. For so it was commanded me by the word of the Lord, saying, 'You shall not eat bread, nor drink water, nor return by the same way you came.'" So he went another way and did not return by the way he came to Bethel. Now an old prophet dwelt in Bethel, and his sons came and told him all the works that the man of God had done that day in Bethel; they also told their father the words which he had spoken to the king. And their father said to them, "Which way did he go?" For his sons had seen which way the man of God went who came from Judah. Then he said to his sons, "Saddle the donkey for me." So they saddled the donkey for him; and he rode on it, and went after the man of God, and found him sitting under an oak. Then he said to him, "Are you the man of God who came from Judah?" And he said, "I am." Then he said to him, "Come home with me and eat bread." And he said, "I cannot return with you nor go in with you; neither can I eat bread nor drink water with you in this place. For I have been told by the word of the Lord, 'You shall not eat bread nor drink water there, nor return by going the way you came.'" He said to him,

"I too am a prophet as you are, and an angel spoke to me by the word of the LORD, saying, 'Bring him back with you to your house, that he may eat bread and drink water.' " (He was lying to him.) So he went back with him, and ate bread in his house, and drank water. Now it happened, as they sat at the table, that the word of the LORD came to the prophet who had brought him back; and he cried out to the man of God who came from Judah, saying, "Thus says the LORD: 'Because you have disobeyed the word of the LORD, and have not kept the commandment which the LORD your God commanded you, but you came back, ate bread, and drank water in the place of which the LORD said to you, "Eat no bread and drink no water," your corpse shall not come to the tomb of your fathers.' " So it was, after he had eaten bread and after he had drunk, that he saddled the donkey for him, the prophet whom he had brought back. When he was gone, a lion met him on the road and killed him. And his corpse was thrown on the road, and the donkey stood by it. The lion also stood by the corpse. And there, men passed by and saw the corpse thrown on the road, and the lion standing by the corpse. Then they went and told it in the city where the old prophet dwelt. Now when the prophet who had brought him back from the way heard it, he said, "It is the man of God who was disobedient to the word of the LORD. Therefore the LORD has delivered him to the lion, which has torn him and killed him, according to the word of the LORD which He spoke to him." And he spoke to his sons, saying, "Saddle the donkey for me." So they saddled it. Then he went and found his corpse thrown on the road, and the donkey and the lion standing by the corpse. The lion had not eaten the corpse nor torn the donkey. And the prophet took up the corpse of the man of God, laid it on the donkey, and brought it back. So the old prophet came to the city to mourn, and to bury him. Then he laid the corpse in his own tomb; and they mourned over him, saying, "Alas, my brother!"

THE NORMALCY OF A CONTEXT

This Scripture is interesting in that it expresses an apostolic and prophetic operation. For starters what draws my attention is that God does not use the local anointing in Bethel, but he sends a prophetic unction from Judah to Bethel and completely ignores that which is local. The context in which we live and the context in which we are raised often shapes and influences how we express the gift of God. Our proximity to the things that God is calling out often makes us oblivious to its obvious error and somehow gives us an unhealthy sensitivity with spaces and places we are called to FIX. This was a common practice amongst the ancients: a stellar example of this is that Lot could not establish righteousness in Sodom and Gomorrah (Genesis 18)

Four hundred (400) Prophets who lived in the chambers of Ahab could not hear God for him, they had to call Micaiah for an uncontaminated word (see 1 Kings 22).

Cities have a way of contaminating us and sometimes we can be so entrenched in its ways and customs that we don't recognize and realize the error because the context has normalized it. The gifts within a region are assimilated into the culture and before you know it, proximity to what God seeks to uproot, judge, and re-establish has contaminated the Prophet where he does not see how wrong it is. It is on the back of this that God sends a prophetic grace from Judah because the local prophetic grace cannot see anything wrong, it is corrupt. What hinders change in a region, is the normalcy of its context.

- Small and insignificant can be normal.
- Poor and struggling can be normal.
- Rebellion can be normal.
- Church Splits can be normal.

There are moments when God will have to send someone who was not raised in the environment to judge it. God sends a Prophet from Judah to Bethel because the prophetic grace in Bethel has become oblivious to that which is God because of the normalcy of a context it is raised in.

Normalcy is first foreign but if it is practiced and sustained over a period of time it becomes the acceptable standard.

God does not trust the old Prophet to speak, He sends a young uncontaminated Prophet to speak because the purity of the Prophet will guard the integrity of the word.

The old Prophets symbolises a season but he has become corrupt and perverted but the young always crave validation, celebration and acceptance and uses the old for their own perverted definition of honour and continuity. The old Prophet needs the young Prophet to maintain his relevance and the young Prophet needs the old Prophet to validate him and that perverse partnership creates a win-win context for them where the integrity and purity is compromised, and they end up using one another. Mammon perverts!

When God protects a grace against mammon and the perversion that governs the established system, separation is always the methodology of building: 1 Kings 13:7-8

Then the king said to the man of God, "Come home with me and refresh yourself, and I will give you a reward." But the man of God said to the king, "If you were to give me half your house, I would not go in with you; nor would I eat bread nor drink water in this place.

2 Kings 4:29

Then he said to Gehazi, "Get yourself ready, and take my staff in your hand, and be on your way. If you meet anyone, do not greet him; and if anyone greets you, do not answer him; but lay my staff on the face of the child."

Galatians 1:11-20

But I make known to you, brethren, that the gospel which was preached by me is not according to man. For I neither received it from man, nor was I taught it, but it came through the revelation of Jesus Christ. For you have heard of my former conduct in Judaism, how I persecuted the church of God beyond measure and tried to destroy it. And I advanced in Judaism beyond many of my contemporaries in my own nation, being more exceedingly zealous for the traditions of my fathers. But when it pleased God, who separated me from my mother's womb and called me through His grace, to reveal His Son in me, that I might preach Him among the Gentiles, I did not immediately confer with flesh and blood, nor did I go up to Jerusalem to those who were apostles before me; but I went to Arabia, and returned again to Damascus. Then after three years I went up to Jerusalem to see Peter, and remained with him fifteen days. But I saw none of the other apostles except James, the Lord's brother. (Now concerning the things which I write to you, indeed, before God, I do not lie.)

God creates a context for purity, but the success narrative of the established system makes us use each other and that is a form of perversion that denies us the purity of relationships, networks, etc.

When men promote you; you owe them, when God promotes you; you owe no man anything but love.

It is my earnest prayer that the revelation contained in this book's teaching would be a source of strength and encouragement to you! Blessings.

LET'S CHECK OUR UNDERSTANDING OF CHAPTER 14: ANOTHER VIEW OF MAMMON

1. What does "mammon" refer to in Matthew 6:24?
2. What is the first level of temptation for a person called by God?
3. How does mammon seek to influence us away from achieving the God given mandate?
4. In what circumstances does mammon gain entry into our thought process?
5. How does mammon hider the work that God wats to address through processing of His Word and His Holy Spirit?
6. What are some of the instances recorded in the Bible where satan uses doubt as a means of jeopardizing God's mandate in a person's life?
7. What are the 4 things that mammon seeks to provide a Believer with in-order to steer them away from their God given mandate?
8. Fill in the Blanks:
   Mammon's strategy of recruitment is h_ _ _ n i_ _ _ _ _ _ _ _y and it a_ _ _ _ _s to the things that men believe makes them i_ _ _ _ _ _r to other men. Men who have w_ _ _ _ _ _d for year with their own s_ _ _e of d_ _ _t, i_ _ _ _ _ _ _ _y, and f_ _r tend to address that, and they tend to become e_ _ _ _ _ _ _t and b_ _ _ _ _s once they get these things.
9. What is the main difference between being exalted by mammon and God?

Chapter Fourteen: Another View of Mammon

10. The author states "God's process purges us of false ambitions and contextualises the assignment in such a way that we understand: The Power, The Glory and The Kingdom belongs to God and not us." Do you agree? Explain.
11. According to Matthew 6:24, how did Jesus frame the relationship between God and mammon?
12. What is the Greek word translated Lord in Matthew 6:24? What does it literally mean?
13. What is the ultimate goal of mammon?
14. Why is it that "No one can serve two masters"?
15. Contrast the Scriptures Genesis 17:27 to Revelation 13:16-17
16. What does the mark upon a servant signify in terms of their capacity to function in a particular system/setting?
17. What is the Greek word translated soul and what does it mean?
18. Based on Scripture, what does the breath of God afford us?
19. What does mammon offer in exchange for our souls?
20. How does mammon operate in top down approach situations?
21. Fill in the Blanks:
    The strength of mammon is c_ _ _ _ _ _g a f_ _ _ e narrative of love when it simply f_ _ _s the lust for r_ _k , i_ _ _ _ _ _ _e, p_ _ _r and p_ _ _ _ _ _m. Love amplified i_ _ _ _ _ _y, lust f_ _ _s the o_ _ _ _ _ _ _n with power, platform, influence and rank. The cost of it all is a c_ _ _ _ e in who you are which leads to a d_ _ _ _ _ _ _ _d identity and r_ _s the individual of sound j_ _ _ _ _ _ _t so much so that the i_ _ _ _ _ _ _ _l begins to b_ _ _ _ e they are the p_ _ _ _ _ a that mammon c_ _ _ _ _d for them.
22. How is the consumption controls narrative linked to the belly?
23. What does culture reflect? How does this affect our ways of doing things and sensitivity towards right and wrong?
24. Do you agree that it is therefore important that God takes us through a harsh journey to remove the appetites we have become insensitive to because of the environment and cultures that we are placed/operate in?
25. What makes satan test and search us extensively?
26. What makes the gifts received from mammon perverted?
27. Why is it that God sometimes must use people from outside of a particular area/setting to speak to a situation?

28. What are some of the things that can hinder what God seeks to uproot, judge and re-establish in a region?
29. When and in what circumstances does normalcy become the acceptable standard?
30. In what instances does God use the methodology of separation for the purpose of building? Explain with Scriptural references.

OTHER EXCITING TITLES
BY MICHAEL SCANTLEBURY

GOD'S ETERNAL PLAN

Let me quote this very important passage of Scripture: Hebrews 11:1-3

> *Now faith is the substance of things hoped for, the evidence of things not seen. For by it the elders obtained a good testimony. By faith we understand that the worlds were framed by the word of God, so that the things which are seen were not made of things which are visible.*

So, this is the premise from which this book would be written. We cannot even begin to understand the Scriptures or the heart of God if we do not believe that He is. And to do that we must enact the faith that everyone of us were given at birth according to: Romans 12:3

Because God always existed, we must understand and believe that He existed outside of space and time in the realm called *Eternal*. I believe that this is why we could understand the following passage of Scripture: Matthew 25:34-40

So, He knew exactly what He was seeking to accomplish, and nothing could take Him by surprise.

And that *time,* as we know it only began when He created it. This was done when He created the Heavens and the earth as recorded in the book of Genesis, when He established the sun and the moon and day and night causing, the establishment of days and night, and the record of days.

UNDERSTANDING THE DUAL ASPECTS OF FAITH

From the onset, Apostle Scantlebury presents the tenets of his tome, by eloquently contrasting the two dimensions of Faith: (1) where we use our Faith to acquire and believe God for new things and victories in Him and (2) where we use that same Faith to resist and battle against all odds that is thrown at us.

After defining the elements of faith, Apostle Michael empowers us with the tools to increase our faith: Our knowledge of God and the application of what we know. It's not enough to know what the Word of God says. What produces real faith is displayed when our actions match our belief.

Apostle Scantlebury gives us an accurate understanding of the benefits of our trials. Contrary to our Westernized belief, Faith and trials are mutually inclusive. We are encouraged to keep trusting God despite the opposition. Trusting God then becomes the substratum of having a pleasant relationship with Him.

UNDERSTANDING THE REVELATION

As we embark on this study, there are certain things that we need to first establish. Here are five things that I believe the book of Revelation is about:

1. Revelation is the most Biblical book in the Bible.
2. Revelation has a system of symbolism.
3. Revelation is a prophecy about imminent events – events that were about to break loose on the world of the First Century.
4. Revelation is a worship service.
5. Revelation is a book about dominion.

Also, we have to study The Revelation as a part of the entirety of Scripture and not as a separate book on its own. It ties in beautifully with the rest of the Bible and Israel's journey. So, as we study the prophecy within this book, we will see how it ties in with Jesus' prophecy recorded in Matthew 24 and many of the words spoken directly to the tribes of Israel. It was a powerful and very relevant book for the First Century Church and gives us today a clear picture of God's way of dealing with His people. When approached from this point of view, fresh realms of understanding will herald some fresh and powerful truths for us today.

Also, we need to bear in mind that the Bible is a record of Two Covenants; the Old Covenant which had a shelf life and was destined to come to an end. And then we have the New Covenant which is eternal and as such will never end. It has been eternally established by our King and Lord, Jesus the Christ. We need to add to this the understanding that the entire cannon of Scripture was written prior to AD 70.

ARE WE LIVING IN THE END TIMES OR THE LAST DAYS?

Whenever we hear this term "end-times or last-days" it conjures up all kinds of images in our minds: from the universe blowing up with the largest flames you could ever imagine! And that it would usher in a new heaven and a new earth. We also have presupposed in the body of Christ that before all of this would indeed occur, the righteous would be raptured away and then the world would be left a massive fire of destruction.

When you hear Christians mention the 'last days,' many just assume it's referring to the end of time and of the world. But the attentive Bible student asks, 'last days of what?' It seems obvious to me that the text is referring to the end of the Old Covenant-Temple aeon/age. When you read the New Testament through these lenses, all I can say is WOW! It makes a significant difference, when you read the Scriptures with the realization that the Bible was written FOR you and not TO you.

We need to also understand that "time of the end" and "end of time" are not one and the same thing. The Bible teaches about the "time of the end" but there is nothing taught about an "end of time."

FATHERS AND SONS – AN UNVEILING

As we embark upon this study, there is something that I would like for us to first understand, and it is this: God the Father is the ultimate Father. There has never been anyone like Him, nor is there currently anyone like Him, nor will there ever be anyone like Him. He is in a class all by Himself.

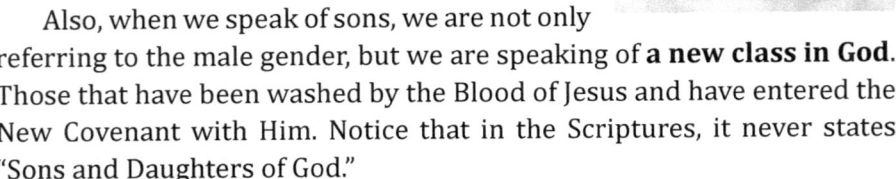

Another thing that we need to understand moving forward is this: Respect produced by force and domination is not respect but fear.

Also, when we speak of sons, we are not only referring to the male gender, but we are speaking of **a new class in God**. Those that have been washed by the Blood of Jesus and have entered the New Covenant with Him. Notice that in the Scriptures, it never states "Sons and Daughters of God."

John 1:12 states

But as many as received him, he gave them power to be made the sons of God, to them that believe in his name. ...

As such, I do believe that women can also be Apostles and in a broader scope, they qualify to "father" should that mantle be upon them.

HEAVEN & EARTH A BIBLICAL UNDERSTANDING

Whenever we today in this 21st Century read about heaven and earth in the Scriptures we need to be careful as to exactly what is being referred to. And here are some reasons as to why this must be.

1. The original Bible was not written in our modern English, which is a far different language than Hebrew and Greek the original languages of the Holy Scriptures. Hence the reason for us to become avid students of the Word of God.

2. We, living today are not the original recipients of Scripture and as such we need to understand what the original recipients understood when they first received that Word.
3. We must be willing to let the Bible interpret itself and not hang on to our theories for the Scriptures.
4. That the Bible speaks of at least four Heavens and three earths. And as such we need to dig deep into the Word of God and find them and apply this understanding in our study.

Remember what the Scriptures say in Proverbs 25:2 *It is the glory of God to conceal the word, and the glory of kings to search out the speech.*

With that said let us now take a deeper dive and journey into the Word of God with the intention of extracting much needed revelation concerning these Heavens and Earths.

MY PONDERINGS

In this book before you the author has been engaged in pondering several subjects and as such, decided to put his thoughts in a book. As you read through these pages may the Lord use his thoughts to both inspire and bless you. Here are some of the subjects he has been pondering, with each one making up a chapter of this book:

My Ponderings on The Kingdom of God
My Ponderings on The Church
My Ponderings on Innovation
My Ponderings on Wisdom and The Power of Vision
My Ponderings on Navigating Seasons
My Ponderings on Breakthroughs
My Ponderings on Unity
My Ponderings on The Many Comings of Jesus
My Ponderings on Eschatology
My Ponderings on Jesus the First Fruit of the Dead
My Ponderings on Understanding the Times
My Ponderings on Understanding the New Covenant
My Ponderings on Gold

UNDERSTANDING THE KINGDOM OF GOD AND THE CHURCH OF JESUS CHRIST

"This book is a game changer and will teach you what it means to be part of This Kingdom."

Pastor Marilyn Bailey
—Teleios Church, Johannesburg, South Africa

"There is perhaps no greater time to revisit the spiritual and practical understanding of the kingdom of God than right now.

Apostle Scantlebury addresses and corrects, common misconceptions, explains the contrasts in the Kingdom of God and the kingdom of darkness, properly aligns the Kingdom and the Church, and propels us toward a holistic understanding of Kingdom life in the earth.

With great patience and clear articulation, Apostle Scantlebury lays out a compelling case for the people of God to give priority to understanding and walking in the principles of the Kingdom of God in life and ministry.

Do yourself a favour; set aside some time to read through and study this transformative volume. You will be challenged, changed, and equipped to be a proper representative of the kingdom of God."

Apostle Eric L. Warren—Eric Warren Ministries
Charlotte, North Carolina, USA

ESCHATOLOGY – A BIBLICAL VIEW

If you were a time traveler and traveled back to the time of say Abraham Lincoln and told him you were from the future in 21st century. What if he asked you how people communicated in the 21st century, and now you had to try and explain say how an email works. How would you explain it?

Would you use something he would be familiar with to describe it? Perhaps you would tell him that in the future postmen would ride

horses at 500 mile per hour. Or you might tell him you could deliver a message by train from New York to LA in less than one day. You're trying to find a way to communicate how "fast" an email really is. But you're trying to do in a way that wouldn't totally blow his mind.

That's kind of the conundrum we have when trying to understand difficult verses in the Bible, especially in themes like eschatology. The prophetic writers of Scripture had to convey God's mysteries in language that their readers would understand.

Fast forward now 2-3,000 years later, and we are reading these prophetic Scriptures through a 21st century lens, and sometimes coming up with all kinds of weird speculative interpretations because we didn't understand what those Scriptures would have meant to a first century Believer, or a Jew living in the time of the OT Prophets.

The book before you plan to delve deeper into this and much more as it seeks to present you with a sensible view of eschatology.

THE RESTORATION OF ZION

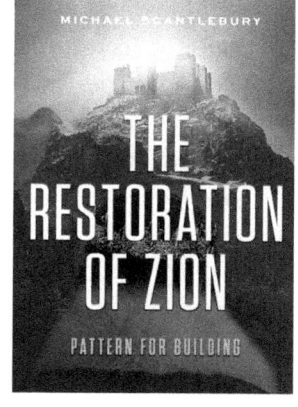

When you hear the word Zion, what comes to mind? As Christians, we've sung the choruses and the hymns about Zion or Mount Zion, but do we fully understand just what we're singing about? Do we know what it is? The Bible promises the full restoration of Zion, and if we don't fully know what Zion is, what then do we anticipate in terms of its restoration?

The greatest hindrance to accurate interpretation and application of Scripture is a futuristic view of Scripture. This futuristic view continues to rob the Believer of experiencing God in His fullness in the here and now.

In this book, we will uncover within the Scriptures exactly what Zion actually represents to the New Testament Believer. So lay down any preconceived ideas you may have, delve into the pages of this book, and let it speak truth to you.

AS IT WAS IN THE BEGINNING SO SHALL IT BE...

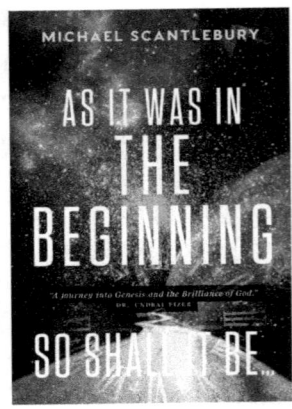

Have you ever wondered about life and all of its intricacies? Why are we here on planet earth? What is out there in deep dark space? Who created it all in its majesty and wonder with the brilliancy of everything that surrounds us?

Since time began, man has tried to explain things regarding the known world. One forward thinker put forth a theory that the world was flat. That was refuted by more research. Study and research and pondering some more have revealed some truth about our world but not all the questions are yet answered.

While many of us as Christians enjoy documentaries on the pondering of the many ways we may have "gotten here" beginning with the theory of alien transports dropping us off, to the idea of a cosmic slime pit which one day came to life, so truly the only authority we have as born-again followers of Jesus Christ is the book of Genesis, the very first book of the Holy Scriptures, which simply states: "In the beginning God created the heavens and the earth." Genesis 1:1

We will broach the answers to these and other questions only God's inspired word, the Holy Bible will answer the many questions at hand.

We will begin our journey into the heart and mind of this incredible Creator to learn the reason and purpose for our existence. And as we take that incredible journey, we would seek to come to terms with the revealed, eventual outcome of our existence and life upon planet earth.

STUDY GUIDE – DANIEL IN BABYLON

This is an exciting study into the present truth lifestyle illustrated through the lives of Daniel and his friends. Whether you'll be meeting with others in a group or going through this book on your own, you've made an excellent decision by choosing to read **DANIEL in Babylon** and studying it in-depth with this guide.

This is a seminal study with strong Apostolic messaging, yet its flowing style allows for easy assimilation of biblical truths, and provides accurate insights for the cerebral Believer, who like Daniel and his companions, are usually the target of the world system. In this book various methodologies are outlined through which, spiritual Babylon seeks to entice the brightest and best of every Godly generation, to acculturize, rob of spiritual identity and manipulate to promote world kingdom end.

PRINCIPLES FOR VICTORIOUS LIVING: VOL II

The initial purpose of the five-fold ministry is for the perfecting or maturing of the Saints, which leads to its next intention, which is the real work of the ministry of Jesus Christ, reconciling the world back to the Father. This book lends itself to help in the maturing of the Saints. It adds insight and strategies that help in achieving exponential personal growth preparing one for the real work of the ministry. This is a volume of information and revelation needed in such a time as this, when maturity and focus are the needed key components that bring us an overcoming victory in this realm and advance the Kingdom of God.

PRINCIPLES FOR VICTORIOUS LIVING: VOL I

The information contained herein is well balanced with a spiritual maturity that keenly stems from wisdom and revelation in the knowledge of Christ. This is the anointing of an Apostle, and the truths that our brother shares will certainly cause you to excel in the Kingdom of God long before this life is over when later we enter the eternals. There's so much to experience today in this life, and Michael extracts so much from the Word of God to facilitate that. His insight of revelation and ability to interpret and articulate what his spirit receives from the Lord are powerful.

PRESENT TRUTH LIFESTYLE – DANIEL IN BABYLON

This is a seminal study with strong Apostolic messaging, yet its flowing style allows for easy assimilation of biblical truths, and provides accurate insights for the cerebral Believer, who like Daniel and his companions, are usually the target of the world system. In this book various methodologies are outlined through which, spiritual Babylon seeks to entice the brightest and best of every Godly generation, to acculturize, rob of spiritual identity and manipulate to promote world kingdom end.

But thanks be to God, there is still a generation in the earth spiritually alert enough to operate within the world system, yet deploy their talents and giftings to bring honour and glory to God. Those with the Daniel mindset will decode dreams and visions and interpret judgements written on the kingdoms of this world in this season.

ESTHER PRESENT TRUTH CHURCH

In a season where the Church co-exists harmoniously with truth and error, this book provides us with a precision tool and well-calibrated instrument of change that is able to fine-tune the global Body of Christ.

The Book of Esther is rich with revelation that is still valid and applicable for the day in which we live. Hidden within its pages is a powerful "present truth" message. The lives of the people involved and the conditions that are seen have spiritual parallels for the Church. Our destiny as the Body of Christ is revealed. The preparations and conditions we must attain to are all similar.

THE FORTRESS CHURCH

According to Webster's English Dictionary "fortress" is defined as: a fortified place: stronghold, *especially*: A large and permanent fortification sometimes including a town. A place that is protected against attack. This book seeks to describe what is a "Fortress Church". We would be looking into the dynamics of this Church as described in Jacob's vision in Genesis Chapter 28, also as described by the Prophet Isaiah, in Isaiah Chapter 2 and as the one detailed in a Psalm of the sons of Korah in Psalms Chapter 48. We would also be looking at a working model of this type of church as found at Antioch in the Book of Acts. Finally we would be exploring The Church at Ephesus, where the Apostle Paul by the Holy Spirit revealed some powerful descriptions of The Church.

CALLED TO BE AN APOSTLE

This autobiography spans fifty-two years of my life on the earth thus far and I have the hope of living several more... Our home was always packed with young people and we did enjoy times of really wonderful fellowship! Although we were experiencing these wonderful times of fellowship my appetite and desire to grow in the things of God continued unabated. I continued to read anything and everything that I could put my hands on that would strengthen my life. I began reading Wigglesworth, Moody, Finney, Idahosa, Lake, and the list went on and on! But the more I read the more this question burned in my heart–"*why is it that every time we hear/read about a move of God, it is always miles away and in another country? Why can't I experience some of the things that I am reading about?*" Little did I know the Lord would answer that desire!

LEAVENED REVEALED

The Bible has a lot to say about *leaven* and its effects upon the Believer. Leaven as an ingredient gives a false sense of growth. In the New Testament there are at least six types of *leaven* spoken about and we will be exploring them in detail, in order to ensure that our lives are completely free of the first five, and completely influenced by the sixth! These types of leaven include the following: The leaven of the Pharisees; The leaven of the Sadducees; The leaven of the Galatians; The leaven of Herod; The leaven of the Corinthians. However, the Leaven of the Kingdom of God is the only type of leaven that has the power and capacity to bring about true growth and lasting change to our lives.

I WILL BUILD MY CHURCH — JESUS CHRIST

"For we are his *masterpiece*, created in Christ Jesus for good works that God prepared long ago to be our way of life." Ephesians 2:10

What a powerful picture of The Church of Jesus Christ–His Masterpiece! Reference to a *masterpiece* lends to the idea that there are other pieces and among them all, this particular one stands head and shoulders above the rest! This is so true when it comes to The Church that Jesus Christ is building; when you place it alongside everything else that God has created, The Church is by far His Masterpiece!

JESUS CHRIST THE APOSTLE AND HIGH PRIEST OF OUR PROFESSION

There is a dimension to the apostolic nature of Jesus Christ that I would like to capture in His one-on-one encounters with several people during the time He walked the face of the earth and functioned as Apostle. In this book we will explore several significant encounters that Jesus Christ had with different people where valuable principles and insight can be gleaned. They are designed to change your life.

FIVE PILLARS OF THE APOSTOLIC

It has become very evident that a new day has dawned in the earth, as the Lord restores the foundational ministry of the Apostle back to His Church. This book will give you a clear and concise understanding of what the Holy Spirit is doing in The Church today.

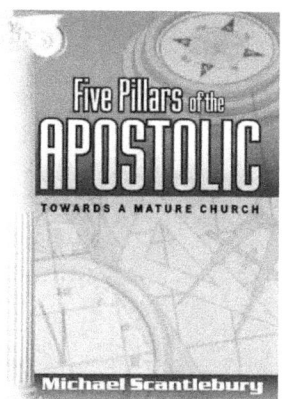

APOSTOLIC PURITY

In every dispensation, in every move of God's Holy Spirit to bring restoration and reformation to His Church, righteousness, holiness and purity has always been of utmost importance to the Lord. This book will challenge your to walk pure as you seek to fulfil God's Will for your life and ministry.

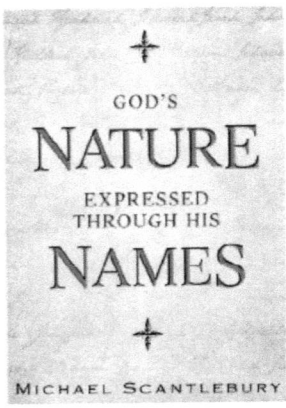

GOD'S NATURE EXPRESSED THROUGH HIS NAMES

How awesome it would be when we encounter God's Nature through the varied expressions of His Names. His Names give us reference and guidance as to how He works towards and in us as His people–and by extension to society! As a matter of fact it adds a whole new meaning to how you draw near to Him; and by this you can now begin to know His Ways because you have come into relationship with His Nature.

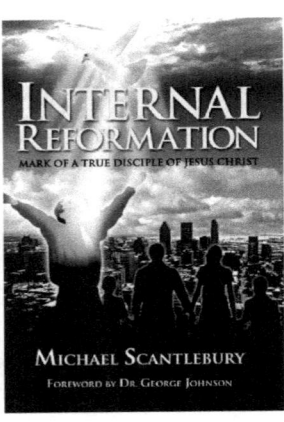

INTERNAL REFORMATION

Internal Reformation is multifaceted. It is an ecclesiology laying out the blue print of The Church Jesus Christ is building in today's world. At the same time it is a manual laying out the modus operandi of how Believers are called to function as dynamic, militant over-comers who are powerful because they carry internally the very character and DNA of Jesus Christ.

KINGDOM ADVANCING PRAYER VOL I

The Church of Jesus Christ is stronger and much more determined and equipped than she has ever been, and strong, aggressive, powerful, Spirit-Filled, Kingdom-centred prayers are being lifted in every nation in the earth. This kind of prayer is released from the heart of Father God into the hearts of His people, as we seek for His Glory to cover the earth as the waters cover the sea.

Other Exciting Titles

APOSTOLIC REFORMATION

If the axe is dull, And one does not sharpen the edge, Then he must use more strength; But wisdom brings success." (Ecclesiastes 10:10) For centuries The Church of Jesus Christ has been using quite a bit of strength while working with a dull axe (sword, Word of God, revelation), in trying to get the job done. This has been largely due to the fact that she has been functioning without Apostles, the ones who have been graced and anointed by the Lord, with the ability to sharpen.

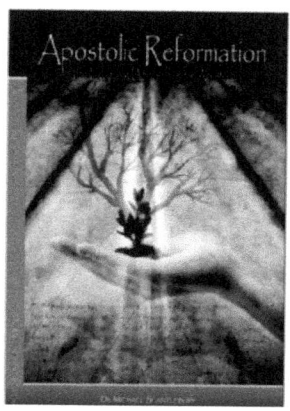

KINGDOM ADVANCING PRAYER VOL II

Prayer is calling for the Bridegroom's return, and for the Bride to be made ready. Prayers are storming the heavens and binding the "strong men" declaring and decreeing God's Kingdom rule in every jurisdiction. This is what we call Kingdom Advancing Prayer. What a *Glorious Day* to be *Alive* and to be in the *Will* and *Plan of Father God*! *Hallelujah*!

KINGDOM ADVANCING PRAYER VOLUME III

One of the keys to the amazing rise to greater functionality of The Church is the clear understanding of what we call Kingdom Advancing Prayer. This kind of prayer reaches into the very core of the demonic stronghold and destroys demonic kings and princes and establishes the Kingdom and Purpose of the Lord. This is the kind of prayer that Jesus Christ engaged in, to bring to pass the will of His Father while He was upon planet earth.

www.ingramcontent.com/pod-product-compliance
Lightning Source LLC
LaVergne TN
LVHW051058080426
835508LV00019B/1943